ROLLING STONES
and the making of
LET IT BLEED

ROLLING STONES
and the making of LET IT BLEED

SEAN EGAN

The publisher wishes to thank the Book Division at Lasgo Chrysalis London for their ongoing support in developing this series.

Published by Unanimous Ltd.
Unanimous Ltd. is an imprint of MQ Publications Ltd.
12 The Ivories, 6–8 Northampton Street, London, N1 2HY

Printed and bound in France

ISBN: 1 90331 877 7

1 2 3 4 5 6 7 8 9

Picture credits:
Cover: © Jorgen Angel/Redferns.
Picture section page 1: Associated Press; pages 2–3: © Robert Altman, www.altmanphoto.com; page 4 top: Fotos International/Getty Images; page 4 bottom and page 5 (both): © Robert Altman www.altmanphoto.com; page 6 top: David Newell Smith/The Observer/Getty Images; page 6 bottom: Everett Collection/Rex Features; page 7: Dezo Hoffmann/Rex Features; page 8: © Jorgen Angel/Redferns.

contents

introduction

The year 1969 was a wretched one for the Rolling Stones. Actually, 1967 is usually considered the band's *annus horribilis*. The fact that they topped and tailed that year with their two most unrepresentative, and to most observers, weakest albums, *Between The Buttons* and *Their Satanic Majesties Request*, wasn't even the half of it. It was the year when the establishment of Great Britain decided to break the band who epitomized and figureheaded a counter-culture that was threatening the censorious and authoritarian values of the old order. Stones vocalist Mick Jagger and guitarist Keith Richards received inflated prison sentences for drug possession, sentences so blatantly discriminatory as to make the appeal courts feel compelled to quash them soon after. Stones guitarist Brian Jones's harassment at the hands of the police was ostensibly less severe—he received no prison sentence—but the price he ultimately paid was far worse: the paranoia and deteriorating mental health partly induced in him by this persecution and then by his failure to obtain an American visa as a consequence of his drug possession convictions (one of which was almost certainly a frame-up) ensured that by mid-1969 (part of the way through the recording of *Let It Bleed*) the Rolling Stones felt compelled to sack him.

Yet a run-down of some of the events of 1969 seems to make '67 pale by comparison.

The year 1969 began, we can only assume, awkwardly for Mick Jagger and Keith Richards. Their friendship—and

7

hence the future of the Rolling Stones, of which they were the songwriting axis—hung briefly in the balance in the last quarter of the preceding year when Jagger had had a fling with Richards's partner Anita Pallenberg on the set of the film *Performance*, in which Jagger was starring. Richards was fully aware of this dalliance, as was Jagger's common-law wife Marianne Faithfull.

Jagger and Faithfull were busted again in May '69 and allegedly experienced sleazy tactics from the police in the process. Joy for Jagger and Faithfull in the summer of '69 when it was discovered that Faithfull was pregnant with Jagger's child (Jagger was already a surrogate father to Faithfull's toddler Nicholas) quickly turned sour. The Archbishop of Canterbury—shocked that the two were unmarried—implored the public to say prayers for Faithfull. This disgraceful piece of moral exploitation and invasion of the pair's privacy was bad enough, but even that seemed insignificant when Faithfull miscarried in November.

Meanwhile, Jagger had other worries. Brian Jones may have been the quintessential pop star heart-throb and a supremely gifted musician, but his increasingly fragile mental state and his inability to tour were major handicaps for a band anxious to get out of a financial hole by going on the road for the first time in two-and-a-half years. They had had their recent differences with the prima-donnish blond guitarist but there still existed a deep bond that went back to their shared residency in Edith Grove, London, in the lean and hungry years before stardom, and Jagger and Richards agonized about what to do. Eventually, in June, they did sack Jones—with the promise of a generous severance package—

and announced his replacement by Mick Taylor. Less than a month later came the gut-wrenching and no doubt guilt-inducing news that Brian had been found dead.

Jagger had also agreed to take the title role in another film, *Ned Kelly*. Faithfull was to co-star. However, when they got to Australia, Faithfull took a massive overdose of sleeping pills in a suicide attempt that left her in a coma for nearly a week and put Jagger on the front pages again for the wrong reasons.

Running in the background throughout 1969 was the Stones' desperation to get out from under Allen Klein, who had become their manager a couple of years before and whom they now considered a man of dubious moral worth and limited financial probity.

While on their comeback American tour during that November/December, the Stones were widely denounced for charging ticket prices far above the norm, a blow to their anti-The Man credentials. Climaxing the tour—and a grisly year—were the lethal events at Altamont, California, where a free concert by the band turned into carnage. Four died, the most awful fatality being the bludgeoning and stabbing of a man by Hell's Angels hired as security in front of the band as they were playing.

A glance at this précis of the year might indicate chaos and misery in the Stones camp, yet '69 is not generally perceived as a bad year for the group. Perhaps it is cynical to suggest that as long as a band is producing the goods musically, the bad things that happen to and around them don't matter so much, either to them or the public, but how else do we explain the fact that '69 ranks well behind '67 in the public's mind as the Stones' most difficult year? While

Between The Buttons and *Their Satanic Majesties Request* merely compounded the Stones' problems of the year they were released, all of the bad times of 1969 seem to have paled beside the artistic triumphs of the single "Honky Tonk Women" and the album *Let It Bleed*.

Perhaps this is because it is difficult to underestimate the achievement of *Let It Bleed*. For, with its December release, *Let It Bleed* marked a significant—even symbolic—milestone in the career of the group: the first time the Rolling Stones had ever put out an album that was better than The Beatles' latest.

That John Lennon somehow always wanted to be a member of the Stones—loving their rebelliousness and hating The Beatles' early conformity—can have offered little consolation to a band who, though recognized as great, were constantly being reminded of their runner-up position in the pop pecking order: the world unanimously considered The Beatles to be number one in terms of both sales and artistry. That the Stones had a tendency toward a monkey-see, monkey-do approach to Beatles records didn't help matters. "As Tears Go By" imitating the classicalism of "Yesterday"; "Paint It Black" the sitar experimentalism of "Norwegian Wood"; *Satanic Majesties* resembling a knock-off of *Sgt. Pepper's Lonely Hearts Club Band*'s carnivalesque tones; the white cover of *Beggars Banquet* following hot on the heels of the similarly blank sleeve of The Beatles' double album—none of these moves broke the image of the Stones as perennial followers, not leaders.

1969 changed that. Though *Abbey Road*, The Beatles' September 1969 release, was a fine album, it marked the point at which the Fab Four stopped developing. Despite the symphonic pretensions of the second side's suite, *Abbey Road* indicated that The Beatles' musical barrier-shattering had culminated in a resting place of pleasant but unambitious generic rock. *Let It Bleed* on the other hand showed a band who were still very much at the cutting edge. It was topped and tailed by two almost perfect epics. The record closed with "You Can't Always Get What You Want", in which Mick Jagger observed with the same sympathetic but detached manner as characterized "Street Fighting Man" the social upheavals of the time (as well as the upheavals of his own private life) to an often awe-inspiring backdrop that featured sweeping musical accompaniment and the transcendent vocal frills of the London Bach Choir. Meanwhile, its opening track remains their greatest artistic achievement: "Gimme Shelter" was a brutal and gargantuan extrapolation of the blues, teeming with apocalyptic imagery and riven by bigger-than-life slashes of mouth harp.

Between those stunning bookends, the record boasted a moving love song (and Keith Richards's first full vocal performance) in "You Got The Silver", celebrations of sleaze in "Monkey Man", "Live With Me", and the title track, a tribute to Robert Johnson ("Love In Vain"), and an atmospheric evocation of a bogey man in the slinky and hypnotic "Midnight Rambler". There was also an intriguing lateral view of their hit record "Honky Tonk Women" in the rustic shape of "Country Honk". (This book, incidentally, will treat "Honky Tonk Women" as part of the *Let It Bleed* album, as it was clearly part of the album's sessions and would have ended up on it had it not been for the then prevailing tradition of stand-alone singles.)

Placing *Let It Bleed* beside *Abbey Road* creates an unmistakable impression of the Stones nudging ahead in the race for the crown of top rock act. (Bob Dylan, the other prospective contender, had deliberately put himself out of the running with the retrograde countryisms of *Nashville Skyline*.) It showed a band rejuvenated by the sense of purpose brought about by jettisoning Jones and recruiting his replacement Mick Taylor (even if the latter did appear on only two tracks). It also saw the band cementing—possibly even caricaturing—its anti-establishment credentials. While the sleaze of "Monkey Man", "Live With Me", and "Midnight Rambler" may sometimes seem like dated schoolboy smut today, their two-fingered defiance of the values of the old social order actually carried real weight a mere two years after the establishment had taken the band so seriously as to attempt their destruction.

Let It Bleed ensured that the Rolling Stones ended the Sixties as they had run their lives throughout them, with a swaggering declaration that the world was metamorphosing into a less severe, less unfair place. They also closed the decade as something that, despite their impressive back catalogue, they had never quite managed to be before: the greatest rock 'n' roll band in the world.

This is the story of how that musical milestone came about.

out of time

After four decades of their existence, the story of the Rolling Stones has a certain grand familiarity. However, it would be remiss to examine *Let It Bleed* without placing it in the context of their history and public image, so a whistlestop tour of their pre-*Bleed* career will set the scene.

We'll dispense with the details of their childhoods. We'll also not recite the minutiae of their years spent paying dues at sweaty venues, except for these comments from Bill Wyman, who explains just how purist and specialist the band were before they became one of the biggest box-office draws in entertainment history. "There was like fifty people in England that knew anything about blues," he says. "If you heard the new album of Jimmy Reed on Veejay or something, someone spent a lot of time finding that and buying that off of some American airman who was posted here or something and they made tapes of it and passed it to each other. Way back in '57, when I first saw Chuck Berry in the film *Rock, Rock, Rock!* he blew me away, so [I] immediately went to my local record shop in south London and tried to buy it. They didn't have anything. Nothing was imported on Chuck Berry. So I had to write off to a record company in Chicago and wait a month to get *One Dozen Berries.* I found later— researching the Stones' history—that that's exactly what Mick did two or three years after I did ('cos he was younger). Young people don't realize that in the early days, they were not available, those records. That's why the Stones were so successful and so different in those days from any other bands in the pop era because we were a blues band playing music that the general public had never heard."

There was a drawback to this. Wyman says, "When you were in ballrooms, they just stood there open-mouthed, gaping, and had no idea what to do to the music." It was only when they realized that promoters wouldn't book them, Wyman admits, that the band moved over from 12-bar blues to rhythm and blues, of which he says, "It's a bit more poppy. It's black man's pop music at the time originally." It wouldn't be long before the Stones effectively became a pop band—for what else can you term chart regulars?—although they would always retain their gritty edge.

Their first commercial release was "Come On" b/w "I Want To Be Loved" (June 1963; all dates herein refer to UK releases unless indicated). Ever since its release, this record has been virtually disowned by the Rolling Stones. Never played live beyond 1964, it was considered such a shameful piece of compromise by the band that it enjoys a status barely above a rather ugly incident from their past that is best not spoken of. Well, it shows how much the Stones know about themselves, for not only is "Come On" a fabulous record but in a way it sums up the group. Unlike the thousand-and-one rhythm and blues combos operating in the UK during the early Sixties, the Stones had an original vision. They weren't content to play note-for-note versions of their heroes' compositions. A Stones arrangement of an R&B or blues number would always be noticeably different to the template, with anything from a little twist in the form of a new lick or vocal phrasing to—as in this case—such a drastic restructuring as almost to constitute a new song. This was what made the Stones the great band they were and what ensured that they would ultimately smash free of the cover-job approach that might provide a living for a couple of years but that, in an age when originality became the keystone for continued respect from the public (measured by sales), could not sustain a career.

For proof, compare the Stones with The Animals. The latter, in the beginning, were a superior ensemble: with Alan Price's mesmerizing organ runs and Eric Burdon's ultra-authentic gravely voice, they sounded like grizzled old men to the Stones' adolescent boys. Yet though The Animals' music had a gravitas that the Stones' early records (fun though they were) did not, it was The Animals who proved capable of nothing more than imaginative interpretations of the compositions of others and the Stones who went on to become a major songwriting force that straddled decades of superstardom.

"Come On" is a breakneck and punchy reinvention of one of Chuck Berry's lesser-known numbers, with the Stones (and Jagger particularly) investing real passion in the song's impatience with the irritants of everyday proletarian life (a subject that makes it a sort of precursor to their own later "'Satisfaction"). The production is credited to Stones co-manager Andrew Loog Oldham but the finely judged EQing cannot possibly be the work of a novice: drummer Charlie Watts's brisk fills, Brian's locomotive-whistle mouth harp, Keith's metallic string stabs, Bill Wyman's intelligent bass work and Mick's belligerent singing are all eased in and out of the mix to optimum effect courtesy of engineer Roger

Savage. The B-side was a respectable version of Willie Dixon's "I Want To Be Loved".

Following the withdrawn "Poison Ivy"/"Fortune Teller" single, the Rolling Stones took advantage of the cachet of releasing a song by the Lennon/McCartney partnership that was the hottest thing in popular music at the time with "I Wanna Be Your Man". released in November 1963. According to Keith Richards (who at the time of the making of *Let It Bleed* was still going by his s-less *nom de guerre* Keith Richard but who shall be referred to as Richards throughout this text), it was the speed with which the pair finished a half-completed number just prior to gifting it to them that first planted the idea in the Stones' heads that composing was not as difficult as it seemed. "I haven't heard it for ages," Jagger said in 1968, "but it must be pretty freaky 'cause nobody really produced it." Jagger is being uncharacteristically modest, for this is one of the few records ever released in which an artist manages to top The Beatles' own rendition of one of their tunes. Admittedly, this throwaway—given to Ringo for *With The Beatles*—was never going to be a classic whoever did it, but, with the band tackling it with unstinting enthusiasm and faith, an unexpectedly fine end-product results. "I Wanna Be Your Man" is a great blurred threshing machine of noise, with Jagger sounding his most indolent and Brian contributing a nosebleed guitar solo. The fine B-side "Stoned"—the first composition attributed to Nanker-Phelge—is a derivative quasi-instrumental. An echo-drenched Jagger intones the title over the chord sequence to Booker T. and the MG's "Green Onions". This was the first Stones single released in the US, where it failed to chart.

Though the Stones might think otherwise, "Not Fade Away", their third single, released in February 1964, is the real joker in their pack. What on earth was a bunch of R&B purists doing covering a Buddy Holly pop tune? By their own criterion, if "Come On" was compromise, this was pure prostitution, though that is not to say it's a bad record. Imaginative as ever, the Stones take Holly's high-energy pop and drop it in a big muddy puddle for the desired dirty and gritty effect, replacing pristine electric guitars with scrabbly acoustic, emphasizing the Bo Diddley beat (actually present in more subtle form in Holly's original) with maracas, and getting Brian to raise the tension with soaring harmonica blasts. The pleasant blues flip is a collaboration between Jagger and Phil Spector, who had been expressing interest in releasing Stones records on his label in America. (The track's publishing credit was "Nanker-Phelge/Spector.", Nanker-Phelge being a collective *nom de plume* to credit songs the whole band (and Oldham) shared royalties on. A "Nanker" was a grotesque face that Brian used to pull and Phelge a flatmate in Edith Grove, Jimmy Phelge) The Stones were inching toward self-reliance. (Interestingly, though "The Last Time" is famous for being the band's first self-written A-side in their home country, it was the Jagger/Richards effort "Tell Me" which achieved that distinction in the States and achieved the respectable *Billboard* chart result of number 24 in the fall of 1964. It was actually the start of a run of hit ballads for the band Stateside that, initially, gave them a reputation there that was almost the antithesis of their later hardcore rocker image.) They were also making incremental sales progress: in reaching number three with "Not Fade Away", they had their first UK top-tenner. It was also the band's first US chart placing, at a modest number 48.

According to early Stones fan Pete Frame (now a successful author), when it was released in April 1964 the Rolling Stones' eponymous debut album surprised the fans who had religiously attended their early gigs. Not a single one of the 12 tracks on this album (daringly released with no title or artist credit on the front sleeve) was familiar from their stage act. Not that this made much of a difference, for the quality of the album was astounding: from their breakneck cover of Bobby Troup's "Route 66" (learned through Chuck Berry) through their unexpectedly surreal take on Bo Diddley's "I Need You Baby (Mona)" to their own respectable dip into the waters of composing with "Little By Little", to the growling closer "Walking the Dog", the band showed an imagination and technical dexterity beyond most of their peers.

As with all Rolling Stones albums up until *Their Satanic Majesties Request*, this album was tampered with in America, a country bewildered by the UK's tradition of stand-alone hit singles, with tracks dropped and substituted on a record that was retitled *England's Newest Hitmakers*. Strangely, this philistine approach often produced more listenable albums than their UK counterparts—or perhaps not so strangely, considering that the inclusion of classic singles and their often almost equally classic B-sides was hardly going to be aesthetically displeasing. It also led to bizarre odds-and-sods albums like *December's Children* and *Flowers* which, being mop-ups of hits, flips, EP tracks, and tracks left off US albums to accommodate hits, had no UK counterparts.

Fine though their opening trio of UK singles and debut album was, it was with their take on Bobby Womack's impassioned dismissal of a feckless lover "It's All Over Now" that the Stones assumed an air of gravitas. With its great reverberating riff and soaring chorus—which carried a note of regret even in its contempt—it had Smash Hit written all over it from the word go. Accordingly, the British public sent it to number one, which made the presence on the flip of the Jagger/Richard original acoustic blues "Good Times, Bad Times" even more lucrative.

In the States, it was followed up by "Time Is On My Side". Never released as a single in Britain, this shimmering cover of a record by Irma Thomas effectively broke the Stones in America. It was brilliantly arranged—with the band providing harmonies for almost the only time in their career—and wonderfully sung by Jagger. His emoting in the line "I've got the real love/The kind that you need" is guaranteed to give a good yank on the heartstrings. For some reason, the band subsequently re-recorded this track in a version on which Ian Stewart was prominent on organ. This second version appeared on the US album *12 x 5*, which itself appeared in the USA three months before the release of its UK equivalent, *The Rolling Stones No. 2*. "Heart Of Stone" (December 1964) was another Stateside-only big ballad single from the band. A Jagger/Richard track, it's an impressive soul number which deserved better than its *Billboard* chart placing of 19.

In preference, in their home country, the band went for "Little Red Rooster", which is possibly the biggest guilt trip in the history of popular music. As if to make up for the alleged compromise of "Come On" and the irrefutable compromise of "Not Fade Away", the Stones decided to follow up their first UK chart topper with a hardcore piece of 12-bar blues in the form of this resurrection of Willie Dixon's innuendo-packed lament. Though it's far from generic—boasting a nice, lazy ambience, great slide-playing by Jones and fine harmonica from Jagger—it's still amazing that this reached number one. Oldham later admitted to chart manipulation, though considering almost everyone was doing this back then it's difficult to see what difference this made. Wyman says, "We released that record against everybody telling us not to on the Friday and on the Monday it was number one in the *NME*. And it's probably the only blues record that's ever gone number one in England. So it just proves the point that there was an audience out there that liked that kind of music." One wonders, though, whether a band not boasting teen heart-throbs of the order of Jagger and Jones would have had similar luck with such uncompromising material.

The Stones' second UK LP was, like their first, issued with no title or artist credit on the front sleeve, though this perhaps wasn't as daring as the close-up of Keith in all his zit-marked glory. Unfortunately, the music lacked a similar sense of adventure. *The Rolling Stones No. 2* was the one and only time during the Sixties that the band put out an album that wasn't radically different from its predecessor. This wouldn't have mattered, had the album not been merely a pale imitation of its predecessor, a failing that was hardly forgivable considering that they were still mainly covering the material of other artists and therefore had their pick of classics to plunder. The sprightly "You Can't Catch Me" and a surprisingly sensuous "Under The Boardwalk" are among the few highlights.

The final piece of the jigsaw for the future pattern of the Stones' career was the February 1965 release of "The Last Time". "The Last Time" may have been outrageously plagiaristic—only the world's top scientists could distinguish its DNA from that of a traditional gospel song (the Staple Singers had a variation called "(May This Be) The Last Time")—but it was a rip-off bearing the Jagger/Richard signature, the first on an A-side in the UK, which was all that mattered. The B-side was another self-generated number, "Play With Fire". Both tracks are a bit overrated—Jones' winding guitar figure on the hit-side skirts tedious more than it does hypnotic, while Jagger's warnings to a slumming female on the harpsichord-decorated flip are laughably lacking in the intended menace—but in terms of the Stones beginning to be perceived as equals of The Beatles and Dylan, the impact of this record cannot be overstated.

In terms of carving out a niche for themselves in the market, what also can't be overrated is the incident in the summer of 1965 that led to Bill, Mick, and Brian being prosecuted and convicted for insulting behavior. The group were already figures of minor controversy. They had the longest hair of any mainstream pop group (unless the Pretty Things count), something which in a ludicrously conservative age made many people's skins crawl. Allied to their unusual disinclination to wear a group suit—they each wore what they liked—and Richards's vaguely menacing, acne-scarred air, it communicated to a public unused to such a sight in entertainers that they were of questionable hygiene. The Stones actually made the news for being turned away from a hotel dining room after refusing to wear ties, with Jagger making tart comments in the press about the way a hotel treated its own guests. This may seem toytown stuff, but it's a reflection of how buttoned-up British society was then that it was also the stuff of headlines. Oldham—a former record-plugger with a nose for the newsworthy—had realized that the unconventional image might yield headlines and thus bigger record sales and a loyalty from a generation beginning to spurn the attitudes of their parents. It was he who encouraged a journalist to run with a story entitled "Would you let your sister go with a Rolling Stone?"

For long-term Stones friend and music journalist—and later Stones publicist—Keith Altham, Oldham's influence was crucial. "The first time I ever saw a photograph of them that arrived on my desk, I thought the Four Stooges had arrived," he recalls. "They had those pudding-basin haircuts, which were kind of like an attempt to do a Beatles almost in the early days, and they just looked silly to me. They looked goofy. It wasn't until later that things got modified and we found out what they did, and I think the hairstyles got modified as well, but they started to look slightly less stiff and waxworky. Andrew Oldham was very instrumental in all that. The thing about those managers in those days was that they didn't have a lot of business nous but what they did have was a bit of flair and imagination and creativity, and Oldham very quickly released that the initial attempt to do a kind of London Beatles was wrong and what he actually should be doing was almost the exact opposite and set them up as an antithesis of The

Beatles and he latched on to that pretty damn quick. I think that was the thing that helped take them up. In those days you became a Beatles fan or a Stones fan and the Beatles were kind of all-round family entertainment. Epstein had taken them that conventional route that every other pop star had ever gone before and Oldham went in the opposite direction, which was a kind of brave thing to do really because by doing that it meant to a lot of people in the business that they weren't going to have a very long career because they were not going to be accepted by the establishment."

Not even Oldham though could have hoped for the results that erupted from the band pulling into a service station not long after "The Last Time" had climbed to the top spot. Stones bassist Bill Wyman needed a pee. The attendant said there was no toilet. It was clearly absurd that such a large facility would not have a public lavatory: he clearly was another of the growing number of people who didn't like the look of them, or perhaps he'd heard about a recent incident when for the only time in their lives they trashed a hotel room. He later said Wyman had appeared to him as, "a shaggy-haired monster." Either way, his pompousness in barking at the group, "Get off my forecourt!" was symptomatic of the petty authority free spirits like the Stones hated. "Get off my foreskin!" Jones jeered back, pulling faces. Wyman simply walked a bit further down the road and urinated against a wall. One of the Stones is alleged to have said, "We'll piss anywhere, man!" Regardless of whether this latter comment was actually made, it summed up an entire generation's perception of the band. (It would have been the perfect title for their 2003 autobiography, actually called

According To The Rolling Stones.) For the incident, Mick, Brian, and Bill were prosecuted and found guilty of insulting behavior and the group's notoriety was set in cement.

It seems perfectly poetic that the band's next single release, in August 1965, was "(I Can't Get No) Satisfaction", a song that seemed like a bellow of outrage at the petty irritations that blighted people's everyday lives. If "The Last Time" was important because it was perceived to be the record that allowed the Stones to haul themselves to the plateau inhabited by the rock 'n' roll gods, the follow-up was actually far more important because it allowed them to remain there unchallenged. Like many that have become sonic wallpaper through endless radio broadcasts, "'Satisfaction" is a song whose brilliance we are often barely conscious of, sometimes to the extent that we have to dredge up our first memory of hearing it to remind us why it has achieved its Gold radio staple status. Try: that leering, lurching buzzsaw riff tearing out of the radio/record player, the shock of hearing Mick enunciate a title line that was surely a double entendre but which he was going to get away with because no one could prove it, that dreamlike quality of his voice in the first two lines of the verses, that yowling, irritated lyric of a kind which simply had never been heard in pop, at a time when the pre-*Rubber Soul* Beatles were still largely moon-ing and June-ing it and Dylan was rolling up his social commentary in clever metaphors—a lyric that, though it took sideswipes at consumerist banality, couldn't even be bothered pretending it was protest rather than an arbitrary state of pissed-offness, a state that was expressed in the gradually rising fury emerging out of those gentle starts to the verses and reaching full voice in the bellowed choruses.

Remember? Stunning, wasn't it? Charlie's pounding drumming and the way Brian's trebly guitar provides a counterpoint to Keith's relentless chainsaw sounds also deserve special mention.

Though the pleasant enough chugging "Under Assistant West Coast Promotions Man" was the flip in the States, the B-side of the record in Britain only underlined what giant aesthetic steps the band were taking. "The Spider And The Fly" is the first time the Stones added to the blues instead of providing a clever variation on it. Here they use the age-old 12-bar medium as a musical backdrop to a tableau that was then utterly modern: a young singer being hit upon by a groupie, and furthermore one who had reached that horrendously advanced age of 30.

The American version of *Out Of Our Heads*, the band's next album, puts "Satisfaction" in true context. That track started out as a soul number, although its roots in "Dancing In The Streets" were completely obscured by its development into fuzztone freakout. On *Out Of Our Heads* (UK release September 1965), the Stones embraced another form of black music with covers of numbers by the likes of Marvin Gaye and Sam Cooke. It's not altogether successful but at least a sign of artistic ambition. The album is more highly regarded in the States because of the inclusion of the iconic "Satisfaction" and its brilliant UK B-side. However, buried on the UK version is a lost classic, the melodically intricate Jagger/Richards original "Gotta Get Away'"

In its catalogue of modern urban grievances, "Get Off Of My Cloud", the October 1965 follow-up to "Satisfaction", was an action replay of the latter song, with high-rise living and officious traffic wardens taking the place of the waffling D.J.s, inane advertising slogans and uncooperative sexual partners that blew Jagger's top in its predecessor. Not that this repetition of ideas matters a jot: "Get Off Of My Cloud" is a fantastic blast of frustration with an anthemic chorus ready-made for air-punching and wonderfully—and surprisingly—liquid guitar sounds. The delicate, thoughtful flip "The Singer Not The Song" reveals that the band could now write classic ballads too.

"19th Nervous Breakdown" (February 1966) shows the Stones in their swaggering pomp. The A-side is all biting sarcasm, references to dysfunctional families (and, indeed, drugs, although nobody noticed at the time), and music whose distortion pushed the notion of listenability to its limits, from its fuzzy-margined guitar lick to Bill Wyman's underwater-bubbles bass playing. If the A-side was sweeping into places The Beatles were at this point only stepping gingerly into (including an L.S.D. reference), on the flip, "As Tears Go By", Jagger and Richards are displaying the propensity they had to ape the Beatles: this number—written for Marianne Faithfull—blatantly follows in the chamber music footsteps of "Yesterday".

Aftermath (April 1966) was an album comprised entirely of new Jagger–Richards compositions. Of course, this wouldn't have been worth a damn had their original songs been rubbish, but Jagger and Richards were not merely songwriters, they were *great* songwriters. "Mother's Little Helper" is a spiffing music hall sideswipe at Valium-addicted suburban housewives, "Lady Jane" a beautiful Elizabethan pledge of devotion from a swain to his beloved, and "Stupid Girl" and "Under My Thumb" fabulous rockers that mesmerize in both their tunefulness and their spitefulness. The extended 12-bar blues of "Goin' Home", meanwhile, illustrates that the group haven't completely abandoned black forms for a beat-group format. The album has its faults: the second half falls away in quality, and like many in the Sixties the Stones seemed to confuse rebelliousness with antipathy toward women. Nonetheless, *Aftermath* is a huge milestone.

It was by now becoming apparent to any objective observer (which doesn't include Jagger, Richard, and Oldham, none of whom could stand him) that, though he hadn't managed to become part of the Stones' composing nucleus, Brian Jones was a genius. What other adjective can one use to describe a man who could pick up any instrument—string, percussion, or wind—and learn how to play it within days or even hours? Having already mastered guitar, piano, and harmonica, in 1966 he would grace Stones records with dulcimer, marimbas, and sitar, and the following year with recorder, flute, trumpet, tablas, saxophone, and mellotron. Though the band could call on outside contributors like Jack Nitzsche and Nicky Hopkins for decorative touches, without Jones' day-to-day presence, it is surely the case that they would not have blossomed in the exotic way they did. In '66 and '67—the years that sealed their reputation as heavyweights—the Stones were creating far richer canvases than before, the imperishable quality of much of their unadorned rock notwithstanding.

A case in point is "Paint It Black" (sometimes rendered with a comma after the first two words), a single released in May 1966, and a far cry from anything the band had produced before this: a mysterious and mordant creation that sees Jagger manic-depressed but in an artistically surreal way while

Watts pounds drumskins treated for a suitably Eastern effect. Jones, however, makes the record. Spurning the standard way of playing the sitar, he strums rather than plucks it to create a unique ambience. It's interesting that, unusually, the narrator doesn't blame his state on unreliable women. The record's unusual non-scathing air is heightened by its lovely (UK) flip, "Long Long While", in which Jagger determines to apologize to a woman he has wronged to a dramatic soul backing. (The US B-side was "Stupid Girl".)

Though they had developed a tradition of great B-sides, the September 1966 release of "Have You Seen Your Mother, Baby, Standing In The Shadow?" was the first occasion when a Stones flip was superior to the A-side. This is not because "Who's Driving Your Plane?" is any kind of classic, though it is a very diverting 12-bar, piano-dominated number cut from the same contemptuous cloth as "19th Nervous Breakdown". Instead, it's because the A-side is a grand experiment that completely fails to come off. The most bizarre thing to which the group ever attached their name (unless *Jamming With Edward* counts), this comes across as half-baked social commentary set to a maladroit attempt at a production in a Phil Spector mold (whom Oldham was at this point almost obsessed with becoming the British version of). It's not exactly unendurable, but an utterly muddy mix means that it is close to featureless. Significantly, it's only when the bombast quits that something close to a hook emerges in the shape of that charming bridge: "Tell me a story/About how you adore me."

The January 1967 pairing of "Let's Spend The Night Together" and "Ruby Tuesday" is in one sense the greatest single the Stones ever released. Just as the Beatles' 1968 coupling of the imperishable ballad "Hey Jude" with the distortion overdrive of "Revolution" showed the staggering breadth of their talents, so the two songs on this release proved that the Stones could handle sleazy rock 'n' roll and pastoral tenderness with equal ease and brilliance. Lyrically, the A-side was simply revolutionary. Propelled by a pounding Jack Nitzsche piano riff, its frank discussion of casual sex—absurd as it may seem from today's perspective— was jaw-dropping in 1967. The track, which topped the UK charts, began that year almost as a deliberate confirmation of the Rolling Stones' outlaw status, and it's perhaps no coincidence that over the course of '67 the British establishment—police, law courts, and the media—did their very best to crush them.

It was possibly the puritanism of America that made "Ruby Tuesday" the side of the record favored by radio stations there, but on balance it's the better track. Jagger's inappropriate American accent has dated it slightly, but otherwise "Ruby Tuesday" is genteel perfection, a heart-aching goodbye to a former lover, on which Nitzsche plays delicate piano while Jones contributes a lilting recorder part. It is Nitzsche and Jones who bring the song to a close, with Jones on his own wrapping it up with a gorgeous, fluttering mini-coda. Jagger has admitted he had nothing to do with this song's composition, which makes all the more plausible the suggestion from some quarters that the publishing credit for this track should have read "Jones/Richards", rather than "Jagger/Richards".

Also released in January 1967 was the album *Between The Buttons*, a very pop-oriented collection that is one of the most uncharacteristic of their entire career. Of course, being the Stones it's a somewhat twisted and edgy form of pop, the pretty tunes carrying lyrics littered with misogyny, drug references, and social commentary. In retrospect, it's surprising that this album is not better regarded. Aside from boasting fine songs like "Back Street Girl" (like *Lady Chatterley's Lover* with the genders reversed), "Miss Amanda Jones" (the only real rocker), and "Yesterday's Papers" (more women-baiting, with a haunting riff), it has a lush texture in marked contrast to the slight tinniness that still prevailed even on *Aftermath*.

The events in the Stones' lives—or at least those of Mick, Keith, and Brian—between that album and their next commercial release are apparently so painful that none of them could bring themselves to speak in depth about them for the *According To The Rolling Stones* book, which devotes around a page to them, most of it comprised of tangential references. The plain facts are that one day in February 1967 the Stones were busted at Richards's country home, as an upshot of which Jagger was charged with possession of illegal drugs and Richards with allowing his home to be used for the consumption of illegal drugs. Their friend art dealer Robert Fraser was charged with possessing heroin. All were found guilty and were given prison sentences: Jagger three months, Richards one year, and Fraser six months. The sentences handed out to the two Stones were clearly discriminatory: even William Rees-Mogg—the ultimate old fogey—was moved to say in an editorial of *The Times*, which he then edited, "There must remain a suspicion that Mr Jagger received a more severe sentence than would have been

thought proper for any purely anonymous young man."
(Bizarrely, Rees-Mogg ignored Richards completely.) A day
after being sentenced, the Stones were released on bail
pending an appeal. Their sentences were eventually quashed.

Meanwhile, Brian was having his own problems with the
drugs squad. In October 1967 he had been sentenced to nine
months' imprisonment after admitting to possessing Indian
hemp and allowing his flat to be used for the smoking of the
drug. He immediately appealed and was ultimately given
three years' probation in December, something that may
have been prompted by Leslie Black—the judge in Jagger's
and Richards's trial—making a joke in an after-dinner speech
about having attempted to "cut those Stones down to size."
However, three psychiatrists had told Jones' appeal court
judge that he was "an extremely frightened young man." That
December, Brian collapsed and was rushed to hospital
suffering from "strain". The following May, he was busted for
possessing cannabis. It was almost certainly a fit-up. Even the
judge at his trial in September '68 seemed to agree with the
implication by his defense counsel that the drugs were
planted, and some observers thought he was displaying
contempt for the jury who found him guilty by passing only
a fine. Jones himself had been expecting a prison term. By
that, time Jones was a hollow wreck of a man.

While Jagger and Richards had been awaiting trial, the
band recorded "We Love You". The last (UK) Stones single
to which Brian Jones made a significant contribution was at
least a glorious swansong for the man who had founded and
led the band but who was shortly to complete his reduction
(in his colleagues' eyes) to an annoying, irrelevant, and

unreliable relic of the past. When it was released after the quashing of Jagger's and Richards's prison sentences, it would feature the sound of banging cell doors and the footsteps of freed men. "We Love You" was the increasingly beleaguered band's message to their fans, expressed in the vocabulary fashionable in '67. This applied not just to the flower-power-informed title but to the music. In an age when groups were shoehorning anything that smacked of another continent into their soundscapes, the Stones outdid everyone with "We Love You", surely the most exotic concoction in pop history up to that point. The result, underpinned by Nicky Hopkins' rippling piano, was majestic—and shame on the U.K. Stones fans who spurned the chance to display solidarity with their heroes in their bewildered refusal to send this single higher than number eight. "Dandelion" was the track favored by stations Stateside.

For Olympic engineer George Chkiantz, this unusually long (4:30) single was Jones's finest hour. The psychedelic epic that one rock critic once memorably described as the "only time the Stones trounced *Sgt. Pepper*" featured Jones playing the mellotron—a device comprised of tape loops imitating various musical instruments, each activated by a keyboard—like it was a conventional keyboard instrument. He chose to use it to replicate Arabian brass. Chkiantz describes his playing on this as a "fucking miracle". He continues, "Hard enough to play that part anyway but to play it on that instrument … Imagine an enormous tape recorder with fifty or sixty tapes and a pinch wheel that goes down when you press a key. So you press a key down and the tape starts moving across the head and of course there's got to be a little bit of acceleration period for the tapes, they're obviously not going to pick up immediately. *If* the tapes were well lined up—big 'if'—that time period would be sort of constant. But of course, they weren't. If the capstan motor had been strong enough, then it wouldn't have varied speed depending on how many keys you had pushed down, but this one did. It was dreadful. The smaller versions of the mellotron were actually better but the big one that belonged to Keith [Grant, Olympic studio manager] had these split keyboards so you had a system by which the left hand played fill bits, so for him to play this part he had to be anticipating the beat by a variable amount. How the hell he got his head into that has always been one of the amazing things in life to me. Actually, as usual with Brian, once he got into it, once he'd sussed it, he did it amazingly quickly. Brian was already in difficulties to some extent but on that particular occasion, he exceeded himself."

To close out a traumatic year for the band, they released an adventurous album called *Their Satanic Majesties Request*, which has been ridiculed ever since as a poor man's *Sgt. Pepper's Lonely Hearts Club Band*. There are only two things that give rise to that accusation: one is purely non-musical—the front-cover group pose in psychedelic finery—the other is the way that the opening track ("Sing This All Together") has a reprise. However, if we rule out the incredibly rich and exotic soundscape as copycat behavior on the grounds that The Beatles didn't have a monopoly on lush, we are left with a fine record with mostly original vision. Though the band look like reluctant schoolboys in a school play on the cover, there is nothing half-hearted about their musical adventurism therein, with songs boasting titles like "Gomper", "2,000 Light Years From Home", and "Citadel", and featuring instruments never heard in Stones music before and unlikely ever to be heard in it again.

More than any other, this was Brian Jones's album: as if to prove that talent bordering on genius, this album saw him creating exquisite and exotic vistas by using the mellotron where The Beatles had had to hire mass orchestration for the same effect on *Sgt. Pepper*. Though they made great music following the artistic decline that afflicted Jones very soon afterwards, the heart grieves at the loss of Jones's talents to the Rolling Stones.

A US-only single from this album was "In Another Land" and was credited to Bill Wyman in honest acknowledgment of the fact that one of the highlights of *Their Satanic Majesties Request* had—apart from Watts—nothing to do with the other Stones: Nicky Hopkins and the Small Faces' Steve Marriott made up the rest of the band. It's absolutely excellent, with a fine melody and a lyric whose exploration of a surreal dream chimed perfectly with the album's exotic ambience. Wyman has often complained that he wasn't allowed to contribute songs to Stones albums (and, indeed, the musical contributions he did make were never reflected in a co-composer's credit), and this track—along with some of his solo stuff—is the proof that the band might have been strengthened by the breaking of the Jagger/Richards hegemony in that department.

This was the first Stones album, by the way, that was not subject to tampering across the Atlantic: from here on in, all UK and US releases would feature identical track listings.

Traumatized by the drug busts, the Stones stopped touring. (By 1967 the top three acts in rock—The Beatles, the Stones and Dylan—had for their own individual reasons ceased to play live.) Meanwhile, devastated by losing control of the band he founded to its songwriting axis, losing girlfriend Anita Pallenberg to Keith Richards, and by the drug police harassment, Brian Jones began his long freefall into the abyss. He barely contributed at all to *Beggars Banquet*, the follow-up to *Satanic* that saw the group return to their bluesy musical roots, an album preceded by the single "Jumpin' Jack Flash".

The lyric of "Jumpin' Jack Flash" is now so well known that we don't think about it, but it's a fantastically weird and grotesque affair with some quite disquieting imagery ("I was raised by a toothless, bearded hag"). The music is appropriately primeval, with a minimalist riff (whose authorship Wyman has claimed) and a general murkiness. The record, if a little overrated, returned them to the top of the charts in Britain and went top three Stateside.

This big, nasty, dirty record was the start of a new era for the Rolling Stones. This was the beginning of their career as the Rock 'n' Roll Band archetype. In the coming four years, their greatest albums would be made, one of which would be entitled *Let It Bleed*.

you can't always
get what you want

"They were an interesting bunch of people," says Olympic Studio staff engineer Alan O'Duffy, who worked on many Stones recording sessions. "Mick Jagger is an extraordinarily bright guy. He could have headed up any international company. He's a bright spark. And Keith is an interesting, great character. He's such a character. A fascinating character and almost a bohemian character. Like a bohemian aristocrat. Lovely guy … [Brian] was a fine-built man. He wasn't a pushover in the slightest, and he was a very flamboyant guy and a very humorous man who I had a lot of time for … Bill Wyman had his character, which is very much straighter and 'Where do I plug in? Here, I'm ready. Right, I'm in tune, here we go.' And Charlie was a fine drummer, a fine musician and great guy who just sat there, without a smile. So from my point of view, I was delighted to have the pleasure of being on their rota and working with them. A privilege. There was no aspect of show business about them. They just got on with it. Musicians are musicians. They're just struggling through and trying to find a groove or a feel for a particular song."

The first recording sessions undertaken by this disparate group of people who, in aggregate, could wield such musical magic for the album that would eventually be called *Let It Bleed* would seem to have taken place at Olympic Studios on November 16 1968.

The months leading up to this date had been hard. The greatest hassle must surely have been the circumstances surrounding the filming of the movie *Performance* (or *The Performers*, as it was originally to be known), which started on September 2. Mick Jagger had taken one of the lead roles as Turner, a still young but already retired rock star living in soporific decadence with two women in a house in London. Into Turner's world accidentally comes Chas, an East End gangster played by James Fox, who is on the run from his former low-life colleagues. Chas initially laughs at Turner's androgyny and effete mannerisms. In fact, one comment he makes to him—"You'll be a funny-looking figure when you're fifty"—is now rather discomforting in a reality where Jagger is past sixty and still rather attached to appearing young and fashionable. But he gradually sheds his conservative mores as he immerses himself in Turner's drug- and sex-induced bliss. It was a fine film, with totally convincing performances by both Jagger and Fox. Many have assumed that the feat of the rather upper-crust Fox in adopting the mien and accent of a cockney thug was a greater achievement than Jagger's portrayal of a randy rocker. After all, wasn't Mick just playing himself? Keith Altham, who was friends with the Stones at the time and got to know them even better when he did a four-year stint as their PR man starting in 1978, thinks so. "It was the only decent film he's ever made, primarily because he played himself in it. Or at least a version of himself." Jagger's lover of the time, singer Marianne Faithfull, has scoffed at such opinions, asserting in her autobiography *Faithfull* that she and Jagger had discussed the character and decided to base it on Keith Richards (for his strength and cool) and

Brian Jones (for his self-torment and paranoia). "Mick's personality was not dark enough or damaged enough to support a mythic character such as Turner ... He's too normal," she wrote, though she added, "A sort of Mick still bled through." She also said, "He did his job so well ... he became this hybrid character and never left it."

It would become a source of no little anguish for both Faithfull and Keith Richards that during the filming of *Performance*, Jagger embarked on an affair with Anita Pallenberg, who as well as playing one of Turner's lovers also happened to be Richards's partner. One can to some extent understand the temptation felt by Jagger and Pallenberg: each was one of the most beautiful specimens of youth in swinging London and large sections of the filming placed them naked together on set. However, even that charged atmosphere—as well as the wider abandon of a public which had only recently thrown off the shackles of propriety and censoriousness that, it was then felt, had always had more to do with the authorities imposing their values on others and the lack of the Pill than an expression of genuine public desire—would surely not have been enough to make most people lose sight of just what an overwhelming, all-encompassing betrayal the affair constituted. Each was humiliating and hurting the two people closest to them in their lives: Jagger was Faithfull's partner and Richards his best friend, Richards was Pallenberg's partner and Faithfull *her* best friend. Furthermore, Jagger and Pallenberg were taking no precautions to conceal their affair. After Cammell had called "Cut" on one bed scene, the two had continued making love—for real—and their exertions were later entered by

Cammell in a continental European pornography festival (without their knowledge), for which they won an award.

The situation reduced Keith Richards—legendarily afraid of no one, and not a man known for avoiding confrontations—to helplessness. His employee and drug-provider Tony Sanchez would drive him to the set to pick up Pallenberg and find that Richards refused to come inside with him. Writing in his book *Up And Down With The Rolling Stones*, he recalled, "He seemed afraid that he would be forced into a confrontation, realized that once he caught Mick and Anita making love he would lose both of them and his world would crumble."

One didn't have to be a prude to take the attitude that if this was what resulted from it, then you could stick Sixties permissiveness. This certainly seems to have been the attitude of Fox, who, traumatized by what he saw on the set of the movie, sought solace in religion, temporarily abandoning his acting career in the process.

Faithfull considered Jagger to be the entirely guilty party. However, her exoneration of Anita ("I saw Anita as very much a victim of all this, the vulnerable one who should have been looked after and protected. Her breakup with Brian over the previous year had been devastating. She already had a hard time distinguishing between what was real and what was imaginary, so it was only natural that she would find Mick's incarnation of Turner irresistible") is counterpointed by the recollections of Sanchez, who said in his book that Anita, referring to the fact that she had graduated from being lover of first Brian Jones then Richards then Jagger, had exulted in her position and declared, "I'm certain that any one of them would break up the band for me. It's a strange feeling." Keith Altham says of Pallenberg, "I was kind of attractively repelled by her. She had those kind of venomous good looks that some women have. She was obviously extremely bright but she kind of frightened me. There were all these things about black magic and the occult that they were messing around with at the time. Not that I think that they were genuinely Satanists or witches or whatever— although Bill Wyman always thought Anita was a witch—but I think they were doing it because it was trendy at the time and Mick was into it because it was dangerous and there was an edge of being smart, sophisticated, risqué, whatever."

Altham spent time on the set of *Performance* in his capacity as a journalist. Asked if he sensed a *frisson* between Mick and Anita, he says, "I don't know that I actually did. I just felt there was little sneaky jokes going on, little innuendos, and nudge-nudge, wink-wink stuff, and I thought, 'Ohh. Bit strange.' And that's all I thought about it." However, he does add, "Cammell was a very dark and sinister sort of character. He sucked the lifeblood out of people with that movie. Everybody kind of cracked up after it. Fox became a religious nut and virtually went into retreat and didn't do another movie for God knows how long. Mick managed to get himself with Anita and nearly broke up his relationship with Keith because of it. There was a creepy kind of atmosphere about it. They were shooting on location in some square in London. I felt very uncomfortable. I couldn't wait to get out of it. It was that kind of a movie. I think the whole atmosphere around it was bad."

In all, the Jagger/Pallenberg situation was a grisly state of affairs, and one which, as well as the emotional turmoil it involved, could easily have destroyed the Rolling Stones as a group. Bands have split over far less. If indeed it was the possibility of losing the band that made Richards decide to avoid confronting Jagger or Pallenberg, then this could only have added to his humiliation. It has been suggested that Richards first began using heroin to blot out his pain in this period, something that ultimately led to almost a decade of smack addiction. The more one delves into the matter, the less it bears thinking about. Ironically, though, it may have contributed to the quality of the album that followed. Altham says of Richards, "I think you can hear him bleeding on *Let It Bleed*. I think a lot of the unhappiness that it caused him went into that record. A lot of the angst. Into his playing. Probably what makes it the great album that it is."

A rapprochement of some sort seems to have been reached by November. Keyboardist Al Kooper would show up on the two days of Stones recording that month as a session player. Asked if there was any tension between the Stones songwriting axis, he says, "It certainly didn't look like that to me. Not at all. I would say that Anita was very 'Keithed'. Extremely 'Keithed'." Though Kooper recalls Pallenberg being present, he adds, "Marianne Faithfull was not there. She was in the hospital." Faithfull was suffering complications with her pregnancy and would shortly lose the baby she was expecting with Jagger.

The pregnancy itself should have been a matter for great happiness, naturally, but in fact it immediately presented another difficulty for the Stones camp and Jagger in particular: it was the subject of adverse publicity unimaginable today. The Archbishop of Canterbury actually implored the public to say prayers on the unmarried Faithfull's behalf. It's true that Faithfull's image had until shortly before been that of a convent schoolgirl, and true that in those days only around one in twelve children in England and Wales were born out of wedlock—as opposed to around two in five today—but even so it was an outrageous act of arrogance and intrusiveness by a public figure. It was this kind of censoriousness and authoritarianism against which the Stones had always been perceived as being the figureheads in a lifestyle battle (which is possibly why the Archbishop made his pronouncements in the first place).

Ironically, it may only have been happenstance that Jagger and Faithfull were apparently destined to be unmarried parents. Faithfull was then still married to the father of her son Nicholas, so Jagger was unable to marry her even had he wanted to. To society at large, however, the situation seemed entirely in keeping with Jagger's perceived degenerate morals. Jagger defended himself gamely, appearing on David Frost's chat show with anti-TV sleaze campaigner Mary Whitehouse—a symbolic clash of conventional and counter-culture if ever there was one—and in response to Whitehouse's insistence on the sanctity of marriage, came up with the check-mate response, "Your church accepts divorce. It may even accept abortion—am I right or wrong? I don't see how you can talk about this bond which is inseparable when the Christian church itself accepts divorce." Jagger seemed genuinely delighted by Faithfull's pregnancy and his impending fatherhood. Although they were both devastated when Faithfull miscarried, their reactions were very different. Jagger threw himself into his work. Faithfull—already dabbling with heroin—threw herself into drugs. Faithfull herself is convinced that the Stones song "You Can't Always Get What You Want" was written by Jagger partly about his dismay at her irresponsibility in this regard (the closest he would come, she says, to confronting her over it).

Al Kooper was and is still not a name known much to the wider public, but by 1968 he was already something of a legend in musicians' circles. Born in Brooklyn, New York, in 1944, Kooper was a naturally gifted musician who could play guitar and horns but specialized on keyboards. He first made his name as a composer, co-writing the US chart hits "This Diamond Ring" (Gary Lewis and the Playboys) and "I Must Be Seeing Things" (Gene Pitney). In 1965, his producer friend Tom Wilson invited him to a Bob Dylan session. Dylan was recording "Like A Rolling Stone". Kooper ended up on one of rock's all-time senses-shredding classics by pretending he was proficient on the organ, an instrument he had never played before. His instinctive musicality came into play: Dylan loved the sound he made and ordered that the organ part be brought up higher in the mix. Kooper played guitar in Dylan's band at his ill-received performance at the Newport Folk Festival that year and can also be heard on his 1966 album *Blonde On Blonde*. Kooper also helped to stretch the boundaries of rock with two experimental groups of which he was the leader, the Blues Project and Blood, Sweat & Tears. In addition, he excelled as a producer. He brought

The Zombies to Columbia Records and in 1968 oversaw their masterpiece, the misspelled *Odessey And Oracle*.

It was through Dylan that Kooper made the acquaintance of the Stones. "[I had] bumped into them maybe once or twice," he says of the situation in 1968. That year, Kooper was exhausted from his production work. "I had just finished producing four albums in a row in America and I wanted to take a vacation," he recalls. "I wanted to go to England. I wanted to shop for albums and clothes and just completely not have anything to do with the studio. So I called a friend of mine in England, a producer [named] Denny Cordell, and I asked him if he could meet me at the airport and not tell anybody that I was coming to England, which he agreed to do. Then when he did pick me up at the airport, he said that the Stones office had called him and that they wanted to book me on two days of recording with the Stones. I said I don't want to do it. I don't even know how they knew that I was going to England. I said, 'I'm just not going to call them back.'" But Kooper seemed fated to work with the Stones. Setting off down the King's Road in Chelsea, he ran into none other than Brian Jones. A friendly Jones approached the American. Kooper recalled, "He said, 'Oh we're so excited that you're going to come play on the record' and then I felt really bad, so I did it. I figured if it wasn't fun after the first day, I'd make an excuse and not go to the second day. But in fact I had a wonderful time and I would have played three days ... I thought that I was actually replacing Nicky Hopkins and as a matter of fact I probably wouldn't have gotten that call if Nicky Hopkins [wasn't] in the States and I was in England."

The sessions took place at Olympic studios in Barnes, on the outskirts of south-west London, which had been the Stones' favored recording venue—at least in Britain—for the last few years. Olympic is still in existence today but bears very little resemblance to the building it was in the Sixties, one that many musicians found inspiring. Pete Townshend, who recorded the album *Who's Next* with The Who not long after the Stones recorded *Let It Bleed* there, once recalled of its main recording room, "It was a great big room—nearly a hundred-foot-high ceiling, like an old film stage. Beautiful Helios desk. Well run: the guy that was the chief engineer there, Keith Grant, was and is still an inspired guy in the way he set up the monitoring."

The great big room Townshend refers to was studio 1, where most bands of the Stones' status would do their recording. Olympic studio engineer Alan O'Duffy (who estimates the height of studio 1's ceiling as more like 70 to 80 feet) says that this did not lead to the cave-like acoustics one might expect. "It was a large room with a very short delay, very short reverb time, so it didn't have a reverb that matched the size of the room," he recalls. "The reverb was smaller because it had absorbent walls, so while it did have an ambience to it, it didn't have a long ambience like you would expect if you walked into a room of that size. It was good for your head, because there's nothing claustrophobic about it, and it was wonderful for recording symphony orchestras and wonderful for recording voices or choirs or big string sections or jazz bands. In terms of the Stones, it was a beautiful place to work and it added to the size of the rhythm section's sound for what we were doing. It would have been great for drums."

O'Duffy says, "Both studios were designed by Keith Grant and by Keith Grant's dad, who was the main engineer. Pye studios had been sorted out by Keith Grant with Bob Auger and Ray Prickett but this was Keith's studio, and Eddie Kramer and also a guy called Terry Brown who went on to work with the Canadian band Rush. I think one of those years it turned over a million pounds, like '70 or '69, which is equivalent to maybe twenty million pounds these days. It was a fantastically successful studio and I was part of that team for those years and very happily too. What remains of the studio today is unrecognizable. It doesn't have any of the original features or charm except for the front door. I think the building was imploded and they kept the outer shell."

A great sound recording facility, of course, is only part of what makes for optimum conditions. By now, six years into their recording career, the Stones had concluded precisely who they wanted around them when recording. Integral to that team was Glyn Johns. Johns—then mainly an engineer, now a world-renowned producer—was a rather tempestuous character whose fiery nature was tolerated by studios (as was his then unusual freelance status) because of his indisputable talent at capturing on tape the sounds that musicians heard in their heads. Ironically, he had engineered the first-ever Stones recording session in March 1963, a demo intended to interest record companies. The band and Johns resumed their professional partnership in 1967 during the recording of the Stones album *Their Satanic Majesties Request*. George Chkiantz, another Olympic engineer, recalls, "They used an engineer called Frank Owen. They were unhappy, not really 'cos Frank was a bad engineer but because he was a bit of a colorless personality, at any rate as far as they were concerned. They insisted on getting Glyn in, who they knew from ages back." Olympic accepted this even though they didn't like freelance engineers working there. Johns would be chief engineer on most of the *Let It Bleed* sessions, with Chkiantz assisting, although Vic Smith took control when Johns had to work in America partway through the recording.

Another production personnel change that took place during the *Satanic Majesties* sessions was the departure of Andrew Loog Oldham. Oldham wasn't just the group's producer up to that point but also their manager. He was the man who had masterminded the band's ascent to stardom, shaped their demographic-delineating bad boy image, and kick-started one of the greatest of all songwriting partnerships by forcing Jagger and Richards to overcome their own doubts about their abilities in that department and compose together. When the Stones and Oldham parted company in acrimonious circumstances, they were losing, therefore, a man who was influential on all areas of their professional lives.

Oldham was not a record producer in the strict sense of the term (despite his Spectoresque ambitions in this period, manifested in the elaborate productions that were released on his own Immediate Records label), but those who saw him work with the Stones have no doubts about his abilities. Alan O'Duffy says, "I think Andrew was a sort of Everyman producer. He was a guy who just wanted to hear, as he would say, the sex. Or the essence of what the band were about. And he would try and channel it. I thought Andrew did a rather splendid job really. On 'Paint It Black' and things, he did a wonderful job which was so raw. Andrew had an idea of wanting to get the exact opposite of The Beatles. He didn't [want] a polished record. He wanted raw sexual energy. Andrew would admit that he hadn't a clue what the control desk was about when he first started as a younger man. But Andrew knew what he wanted to hear and had a drive about him and an energy about him that was unsurpassed. Andrew's a very bright and encouraging man and a great producer in my opinion." Dave Hassinger, who engineered key Stones recording sessions at R.C.A. studios in America (including the one that produced their definitive single "Satisfaction"), observes, "I think Andrew was really good because he knew when not to get involved. He didn't interfere. I think that Andrew had an uncanny understanding of the Rolling Stones. I remember one thing we did: that long piece called 'Goin' Home' [Aftermath]. That was only supposed to be around three minutes, something like that. I was going to hit the talkback after they'd gone into this riff and he said, 'No— let 'em go.' He knew when it was happening and when it wasn't happening."

Nonetheless, when the band decided to engage the services of Jimmy Miller on the follow-up to Satanic, they were for the first time dealing with a producer in the conventional sense. Not that conventional was a word easily applied to Miller. "Jimmy Miller was an extraordinary fellow," recalls O'Duffy. "He was the son of an impresario who booked Elvis into Las Vegas, so as a child he would have met Elvis and been around the Las Vegas showbusiness scene really. Jimmy Miller was a marvelous fellow. He was [6' 2"] but had quite small hands and small feet, so he had this wonderful gait about him. He stood bolt upright and sat tall and he rode horses and he was a marvelous fellow with flowing locks and very interesting and funny and entertaining in his own right. And a marvelous drummer and a marvelous percussionist. A marvelous chap, a wonderful, entertaining, enthusing man … He was a great fellow to have in a studio. He was from a different planet in a way. He was a Californian boy and a horse-rider and an athlete and a fit man and he'd pretend to do cocky moves in the control room and he'd dance around. He was hilarious … I think Jimmy Miller was managed by [Island MD] Chris Blackwell and came over from Las Vegas or from LA and worked with Traffic and also worked with Jackie Edwards for Island records … I think it must have been through Chris Blackwell that Jimmy Miller got to work with the Stones."

"Tall, imposing, and very inspiring to work with," is Smith's verdict on Miller. "There were several producers I worked with during that period that became great mentors for me towards my development as a producer later on in my career: Jimmy, Paul McCartney, George Harrison, and Denny Cordell, who was producing Joe Cocker, were producers that had a very strong picture in their heads of exactly the sound concept they were looking for and in the recording process would allow the engineer creative freedom. They would employ an engineer very much for the artistic creation of their own work. When we were recording 'Honky Tonk Women,' for instance, Jimmy was in the studio playing cowbell standing next to Charlie Watts and the cowbell was ambiently picking up on the drum mikes. As the engineer, you are then left to control the session alone from inside the control room, which then gives you a greater importance in your role as a sound creator. Previously in my role as an engineer at the Decca studios, producers were more inclined to direct you as if they had a baton and they were conducting the recording session, so this new-found creative freedom in my work was well accepted by me."

George Chkiantz was less overwhelmed by Miller's abilities. "Andrew very much attempted to control the thing," he says. "He'd be the loudmouth. Jimmy wasn't really quite strong enough. I always thought Jimmy Miller's enormous problem with the Stones was that he was a Stones fan before he became their producer and he couldn't cope with it. He found it very, very, very hard. Jimmy wasn't a tough producer. He found it very difficult to contradict, to push his opinion over people that he admired beyond all measure. I think the strain of that in the end did him in. It was difficult for him and therefore he was obviously trying to find corners where he could make a difference without pushing the Stones around too much. It was tough. It was hard work because you kind of had endless, endless fighting for the drum sound, fighting for the this, fighting for the that. Jimmy Miller especially changed things in detail that I just couldn't see it, really. But in the end we got very good sounds and I think it's always a fight."

"It's nothing like it used to be with Andrew Oldham," Stones roadie (and original keyboardist) Ian Stewart told a journalist at the end of 1969. "Andrew would walk in and take over everything. Jimmy is more of a link man between the group and the control room and he's great."

Of course, the Stones being rock royalty, they had production ideas of their own that they were not shy about expressing. "Mick was very strong in that respect," recalls Smith. "He knew very much what he was looking for." And Keith? Smith says, "I felt more Mick but it was very evident that Mick and Keith were always around on the mixes and always more present in the control room than any other member of the band." Chkiantz adds, "I don't think Keith really relished sitting in the producer's chair. I think he felt slightly awkward on the odd occasion when he did it. I don't think it was his scene and he happily left that to Mick. But on the other hand I always felt if Keith said something, Mick obeyed. The argument just dissipated. Keith is in some ways very quiet but he's a very forceful personality. Mick was a loudmouth but when Keith said, 'No,' it was 'No.' It was quite funny but I can remember Keith lying behind the desk at Olympic apparently asleep. [Mick] was going on about trying to get somebody to play something or other. This one eye suddenly opened like a lizard and Keith said, 'No,' and suddenly it was all forgotten." Just after *Let It Bleed* was finished, Ian Stewart said, "Mick usually sits in the studio itself—he prefers it like that—otherwise he'd probably be producing it himself."

November 16 was given over to the recording of "You Can't Always Get What You Want." Al Kooper thinks that the lyric was broadly finalized even at this early stage of the album, "There were a couple of changes eventually, when I heard the final record, but not many." He continues of that first session, "I got a call from Mick at my hotel and he said that they're gonna come get me about eight o'clock [in the evening] in the lobby so I went down in the lobby and I was quite surprised that it was Mick and Keith that picked me up.

I thought that was nice. I was very flattered." Kooper also noticed that Jagger's normally brown hair was instead dyed jet black, something it turned out had been done for his role in *Performance*.

Though it had been Brian Jones who got him on the session, Kooper was surprised to find that, despite being present, the guitarist took no part in the recording. Kooper says, "He didn't participate at all musically. He lay on his stomach on the floor of the studio and read an article on botany, as a matter of fact." Jones's inclination to employ his sublime musical gifts on Stones records had increasingly ebbed in the past couple of years. "The general opinion was that he was on his way out of participating, but then when you got to see it first-hand, it was interesting," says Kooper. "He had a driver that was there the whole time, just waiting for him. Somebody that was waiting for him with a car."

This scenario raises an intriguing possibility. As a multi-instrumentalist, Kooper was one of the few rock players who could begin to match Jones's felicity with a range of instruments, and in a sense he would have been a good choice to replace Jones when he was fired the following year. In retrospect, does Kooper feel he was being felt out for the role of Jones' successor? Kooper laughs at the question, saying, "I would never have thought that. I had come from a background of being a big session player after playing with Dylan. After 'Like A Rolling Stone,' I got called for tons of sessions and I played on tons of sessions, so that's what I thought. I didn't think they were going to ask me to join the Rolling Stones. That never crossed my mind." Kooper also adds, "There didn't seem to be any tension between Brian Jones and anybody else at that session. He just seemed like a friend that was hanging out. But he was in a good mood and nobody [was] saying anything behind his back or anything like that. He was quite comfortable, in fact."

Kooper recalls some or all of the band's women being present—except Faithfull—as well as percussionist Rocky Dijon, producer Jimmy Miller of course, and, working on his first Stones session, engineer Andy Johns, brother of Glyn. Glyn Johns was actually in America at this point, the first of his two absences over the course of the following year that compelled the band to employ several different engineers on *Let It Bleed*. Dijon, real name Rocky Dzidzornu, had been previously employed by the Stones on "Citadel" (*Satanic Majesties*), "Child of the Moon" (flip of "Jumpin' Jack Flash"), and "Factory Girl" (*Beggars Banquet*).

"I thought they were extremely well versed in how to make a record," says Kooper of the Stones. "Mick and Keith might pass out a bunch of acoustic guitars and they played the song and everybody kind of played along learning the song and they talked about what instrument I was going to play." The teaching of the song to those in the room who didn't know it—i.e., everyone except Jagger and Richards—was done in a happy atmosphere. Kooper saus. "There was a lot of marijuana being smoked, I will say. I was quite amazed at the talent of Rocky Dijon, the percussionist. He could play congas and roll joints at the same time. I wasn't a fan of drugs and recording in an overall view but marijuana does relax you, I will say that." Wyman and Watts were left to work out their own parts. Kooper remembers. "Nobody was told anything. Just played the song and they played along until it got right. Everybody was comfortable … The whole thing was casual. There was not a lot of strictness going on there. Everybody knew what they were doing and I was quite glad about that because I certainly had been in sessions where people didn't know what they were doing."

As the musicians tried to feel their way into the song, Kooper came up with a significant contribution in the form of the bobbling, almost samba-esque percussive rhythm that can be heard at several junctures in the finished track. Kooper explains, "At the time, my favorite record was a version of 'I Got You Babe' by Etta James that was cut at Muscle Shoals studios in Alabama and it had an amazing groove on it. The groove from that record kind of fit this song. So I said to Keith, 'I have this groove from this record that I love. I think it fits the song. I'd like to play piano on the basic track and then overdub organ after we get the basic track.' He said, 'Well that's fine.' So I started playing the groove and he really liked it."

Kooper was not overwhelmed by the methodology of his fellow producer Jimmy Miller. "To my eye, he didn't really add anything," he says. "It seemed to me that Mick and Keith were producing the record … with an emphasis on Mick. When you see that a record was produced by someone, you really don't know what they did unless you were at the session. You don't know if they were a great producer or if they're a lucky person." Kooper's estimation of Miller went down even further when Miller, apparently frustrated in his attempts to obtain the drum sound he envisaged for the track, approached Charlie Watts. Kooper recalls, "Charlie was having difficulty playing the part that he wanted him to play so Jimmy said, 'Can I sit at the drums for a minute and I'll show you exactly what it is.' And he sat down and he played it for Charlie and

Charlie said, 'Well why don't you just play it?' and didn't play drums on the take. He did it with no emotion whatsoever but I thought it was a terrible thing that Jimmy Miller did because at the time I was a producer and I would never do that, especially to someone so immensely talented." Kooper says that one way or another Miller seemed determined to be on the track and that it would have made no difference how well Watts had played. "I don't think Charlie was doing anything wrong and I think he came up with something that he knew would be difficult for Charlie to play and he kind of foisted that on him and Charlie, in a very dignified way, said, 'Well why don't you just play it.' Now, most people would say, 'Well why don't *you* just fucking play it?' and storm out but he didn't do that. He was a different kind of person and in fact he stayed. He was there the whole time."

If Watts was angry but disguising it, time seems to have mellowed him. In *According To The Rolling Stones*, he stated that Miller wasn't a great drummer but great at playing drums on records. He went on, "Jimmy actually made me stop and think again about the way I played drums in the studio and I became a much better drummer in the studio thanks to him … One sixth of those songs is Jimmy for me … Jimmy taught me how to discipline myself in the studio."

The basic track of "You Can't Always Get What You Want" consisted of Miller on drums, Kooper on piano, Dijon on congas, Wyman on bass, and Richards on acoustic guitar. Mick sang along with the track, although this probably wasn't intended for or used on the song's master. As Vic Smith explains of Jagger's vocal methodology, "We nearly always used to try have a vocal mic set up in a side room which would [be used for] a guide track but the final vocals were always performed in the big room as an overdub and artists of that caliber were always experimenting and maybe singing it sixty, seventy times."

At some point, refreshments were called for. Kooper, who was used merely to snatching a cheeseburger and some Coke in a plastic cup in the refreshment breaks in American studios, was amazed at the feast ordered by the Rolling Stones. "They had two vans pull up and lay out a spread of food the likes of which I had never seen at any session I had ever played on," he says. "It was amazing. I was so impressed."

Though "You Can't Always Get What You Want" would ultimately become a lush, multi-layered extravaganza (and the longest Stones studio recording to this day apart from "Goin' Home"), Kooper says that in no way did it initially come across as something destined to be an epic. Only with the basic track completed and the adding of overdubs did things begin to assume an air of grandeur. Kooper says, "We did an overdub where Keith put on the electric guitar and I played the organ at the same time … We were [improvising] and we both had a good little turn … That was a lot of fun and that kind of changed it a lot when those two things went on the track. That brought it up a few notches. And I said to Mick that night, 'If you ever decide that you want to put horns on this, that would just be the icing on the cake in terms of where I got the piano part from.'"

Eventually—and belatedly—Jagger would take Kooper up on his offer but at the time the assumption by the Stones seems to have been that the track was just about done, for on Kooper's second day of recording there was no attention paid to "You Can't Always Get What You Want" at all. Instead, energies were focused on overdubs on "Memo From Turner", a track earmarked for the soundtrack of the *Performance* movie. As only overdubs were required, Watts and Wyman were not present. Nor, to Kooper's recollection, was Miller, with only Andy Johns accompanying himself, Jagger, and Richards in the studio.

According to some sources, it was partly the promise of a soundtrack supplied by the Rolling Stones that ensured the initial funding for the *Performance* movie. The affair between Jagger and Pallenberg scuppered this. "Keith just refused to get down to it," Philip Norman's book *The Stones* quoted director Donald Cammell as saying. "I kept asking Mick, 'Where's the goddamn song?'" According to Norman, "Memo From Turner"—though credited to Jagger/Richards—was actually a collaboration between Jagger and Cammell, an unlikely compositional pairing born out of necessity. It was the Stones who originally attempted to record it but Cammell claimed that Richards tried to sabotage the track again, "With Keith against it in the studio, the song sounded just awful—still and lifeless." Jagger recruited a stellar line-up of musician friends to try for a better version, including Ry Cooder and Traffic's Steve Winwood and Jim Capaldi, and it was this version that ended up on the *Performance* soundtrack, also released as a Mick Jagger solo single.

It's difficult to assess what stage in this fraught process Jagger and Richards had reached the evening Kooper worked on the track. Going by Cammell's claims to have co-written the song, then the affair with Pallenberg and Keith's distressed reaction to it had already happened, as the song obviously already existed. Yet Richards's attitude to the song, according to Kooper's recollections, bore no sign of the sabotage, or at the very least the obstinacy, that Cammell mentions.

"Memo From Turner" is the great lost Rolling Stones classic. Whatever its provenance, the song boasts a superb lyric, and its androgyny, playful lustiness, and sleaze bear the Jagger imprimatur, especially of this period. It's not known whether it was ever considered for *Let It Bleed*, but the fact that it didn't end up on the album is a big pity. The main flaw in *Let It Bleed* as an album is that the lyrics on several songs are almost juvenile attempts to shock which are worlds removed from the decadent but intelligent words to "Memo From Turner". There were two different versions of "Memo From Turner" legally released. The other was on *Metamorphosis*, an album of Stones discards released in 1975 to settle legal claims by their now long-gone manager Allen Klein. The lyric differs subtly on each, but the *Performance* version is the one we will deal with, as it was clearly felt by the artist(s) to be the superior take.

The opening verse makes the listener feel like he has dropped in on the middle of the conversation between characters in a Tennessee Williams play (albeit with a particularly sleazy bent):

Didn't I see you down in San Antone on a hot and dusty night?
We were eating eggs in Sammy's when the black man there drew his knife.
You drowned that Jew in Rampton as he washed his sleeveless shirt,
You know, that Spanish-speaking gentleman, the one we all called "Kurt".
Come now, gentlemen, I know there's some mistake.
How forgetful I'm becoming, now you fixed your business straight.

The action then moves to West London (and a road that is actually within spitting distance of the Westway, the flyover that the Clash would make a rock 'n' roll landmark a decade later), as Jagger speaks of seeing the person he was addressing in Hemlock Road in 1956, a time at which he remembers him being a faggy little leather boy with a smaller piece of stick. Jagger then proceeds to drool over his hunky body on which the sweat glints attractively, before implying the person is impotent. It's back to the States for the next verse, which ends with an utterly grotesque image that name checks a novel by William Burroughs. The reminiscence has moved on to 1965 and a Coke convention, where the person addressed, presumably the same one, is now a "misbred, gray executive." "You're the man who squats behind the man who works the soft machine," sings Jagger.

Following the brilliantly economic and evocative scene-setting of the first three verses, we are then presented with two generalized verses that are no less powerful in their ability to leave us with a vague feeling of disgust, Jagger invoking images of old men doing the fighting while the young men all look on and young girls who "eat their mothers' meat from tubes of plasticon."

Despite the claims against Richards of non-cooperation, a lot of work seems to have been done on this song, for the two officially released versions do not—according to Kooper himself—feature Al Kooper's handiwork. Kooper played not keyboards but guitar at the session he attended. "Actually I suggested it," he says, "because I believe it was something that would have been good where you tuned the guitar to open G tuning and I thought that I could do a good job like that so I asked if that was possible. And they did that and we had quite a good time, Keith and I, playing together." Again, the pair were improvising. "It was a lot of fun. We just fiddled around until it felt good." Kooper's comments on the open G tuning are very interesting in light of the subsequent assumption that it was Ry Cooder who introduced the Stones guitarist to this. Says Kooper, "It's kind of a blues thing and in fact Keith eventually modified it as time went by. He plays on 'Honky Tonk Women' in open G tuning except that he removes the lower string and just plays it as a five-string guitar. And he's become quite classic for doing that."

Kooper himself says of the already recorded track on which he overdubbed, "I assumed that it was the Stones [on the track] and nobody said anything different to me." To the best of his recollection, there was already a Jagger vocal on the track when he began overdubbing with Richards. A version of "Memo From Turner" available on the collector's circuit may be the one that features Kooper. It is slower, more supple and more sensual than the two officially released renditions, and has maracas in the background.

There have been rumors of a track recorded at these sessions called "Rolls-Royce And Acid" which may have been written by Stones friend and occasional sessioner Jack Nitzsche, but Kooper says, "Not when I was there. We only did those two songs."

This was the last Stones recording session of the year. The rest of 1968 would be devoted to promoting *Beggars Banquet*, which, though already almost ancient history to the group, was finally seeing the light of day after a dispute with the record company about its cover, and to *The Rolling Stones Rock And Roll Circus*, which was conceived as a way of presenting themselves to the public in light of their inability/unwillingness to tour.

The reason for the hold-up in releasing the album now seems archaic. For the cover, the Stones had come up with a design—if that's not too grand a term for scrawling the tracklisting, credits and examples of lavatorial humor on a toilet wall—that their record label Decca deemed distasteful and refused to issue. The Stones were as incensed as any figurehead for the new generation would be when stymied by a plank of the censorious and starchy age group whose values they wished to overthrow. Certainly the sleeve, if issued at the time, would have been breathtakingly daring and rebellious. Even by 1968, a certain decorum was still maintained on the sleeves of rock records. The sight in a record store's album racks of a graffitied, filthy toilet (with the word "shit" clearly visible, albeit smudged) would have been truly shocking. Its rebellious spirit would also have been utterly in tune with the times. It's a measure of how much the Stones' generation—partly led by the Stones—changed the world that now it almost looks as though Decca were right. So commonplace are smutty images in the mainstream media that the spirit behind the sleeve has been devalued and the image now looks utterly low-rent. The tasteful white invitation card design in which the album was finally released looks far more attractive to contemporary eyes (although it is the Stones' intended original design that can now be found on C.D.s). This cutting-edge rebelliousness turned by age to infantile muck characterizes the lyrics of several tracks on *Let It Bleed*, whatever the album's considerable strengths.

you got the silver

Beggars Banquet—and "Jumpin' Jack Flash", the single recorded at its sessions but not included on the album—were a rebirth for the Rolling Stones.

Twice in their career, the Stones were visibly shaken by adverse comment. The second occasion was during the heyday of punk in the late Seventies, when the disdain of young musicians who had idolized them before their slide into artistic inertia gave them a kick in the pants and led to the brilliant *Some Girls* album. A similar process occurred almost exactly ten years earlier, following the (frankly unwarranted) ridicule that greeted *Their Satanic Majesties Request*. Shedding the flower-power trappings that had sat far less convincingly on their shoulders than on The Beatles', the Stones embarked on a return to their roots. *Beggars Banquet* saw the Stones re-embrace the blues. They were now far too artistically sophisticated and imaginative, of course, to go back to simple 12-bar patterns. Instead, they used the gritty and earthy nature of the blues as a springboard. Though they were keen to adopt the metallic hard rock roar that was becoming fashionable in 1968, numbers like the epic "Sympathy For The Devil" and the jail-bait celebration "Stray Cat Blues" were the exception. Instead, the flavor of *Beggars Banquet* is mainly acoustic, whether it be tenderly so ("No Expectations") or hornily so ("Parachute Woman"). There's some also fashionable social commentary, appropriate for a year whose backdrop was youth riots in both western and eastern capitals, growing anger about the Vietnam war, assassinations of political figures considered to be counter-culture-friendly in America, and endless street demonstrations. Revolution—or at least civil war—seemed just around the corner on more than one continent. The Stones, as counter-culture figureheads, included several songs in tune with this restless Zeitgeist even if, on close examination, numbers like "Street Fighting Man" and "Jigsaw Puzzle" reveal Jagger to be placed above the fray, observing rather than making a political commitment. The anthemic celebration of the proletariat "Salt Of The Earth", while moving, was really too generalized to be termed political. Nonetheless, the patina of politics—plus the cast-iron anti-establishment credentials that their imprisonment had bestowed on them—made the band seem in tune with the extraordinary times and only added to the favorable reception to the album.

The album was not only artistically brilliant but proved an audience could grow up with a band. The Beatles' eponymous album [the *White Album*] of that year still had enough good-time vibes and pop mentality to satisfy those of a teenybop mindset, but *Beggars Banquet* was uncompromisingly adult. Even Brian Jones—hostile toward Jagger and sometimes Richards, and whose only significant contribution to the record was the sweet slide guitar in "No Expectations"—"genuinely dug" the album according to Tony Sanchez. That the demonic and anthemic "Jumpin' Jack Flash" itself was a hit was no doubt something of a relief for the band after the public had the previous year embarrassingly failed to show solidarity with the recently released jailbirds by sending "We Love You" to number one.

O'Duffy says he wasn't surprised at how hard-core bluesy *Beggars Banquet* turned out to be, "I had always seen the Stones myself as a rhythm and blues band who went commercial. Brian had an idea of having the band as a blues band and they were taken in other directions. Also Ian Stewart was very interested in them being a blues band, a honky-tonk band. Ian was into boogie. I think they were trying to discover their roots, or maybe trying to discover other people's roots. But the band were trying to sort of get to the kernel of what the band were about. And maybe also to define their writing and take their experiment a little bit further. Mick Jagger was wanting to pursue the essence of the band and at the same time make it commercial. He was interested in the earthiness of it."

On December 10, the Stones and an army of others began the two-day rehearsals and filming of *The Rolling Stones Rock And Roll Circus*. It was an ambitious project, involving the Stones and several of their contemporaries performing for a specially invited live audience. Everybody was dressed in a big-top style and there were filmed conversations between the participating musicians. For ambitious, some would say foolhardy: the Stones had last played a live date in May 1968 at the *NME* poll-winners concert and before that in April 1967. For a band so rusty to put on the best performance out of a star-studded bill that included Jethro Tull, Taj Mahal, Marianne Faithfull, and a supergroup comprised of John Lennon, Eric Clapton, Keith Richards, and Mitch Mitchell was unlikely. Then there was the state of Brian Jones. Keith Altham, there in his capacity as a journalist, recalls, "He was fading fast at that stage. He looked like, as Mr Richards memorably described him some years later, a ghost leaving a séance." Nonetheless, in perhaps his last hurrah for the band, Jones replicated his pretty slide part on "No Expectations".

Interestingly, the Stones took the opportunity at their Circus performance to debut the recently recorded "You Can't Always Get What You Want". As with other songs they performed that night—"Jumpin' Jack Flash", "Parachute Woman", "No Expectations", and "Sympathy For The Devil"—they actually ran through it more than once, in order to ensure the optimum rendition for the T.V. program. (The finale of the program was "Salt Of The Earth", which the Stones and friends sang live over the *Beggars Banquet* original's backing track.) The version of the song they performed that evening would not bear more than a passing resemblance to the ornate extravaganza it had become by the time it saw its release on *Let It Bleed* a year later.

In the end, it was The Who who upstaged the Stones, knocking out a tight set that included all of the mini-rock opera "A Quick One While He's Away" from their *A Quick One* album, propelled relentlessly by Keith Moon's staggeringly rapid-fire drumming. In any event, for Altham there were fundamental flaws about the whole project bigger than the Stones being shown up by their support. "[Jagger] looked a prat, let's face it," he says of the vocalist's ringmaster costume. "I mean they all looked a bit strange. But the only one that somehow managed to hang on to a bit of dignity was Charlie. I don't know quite how he did it, dressed up like he was, but he did. They couldn't quite crack it with it because it needed humor and the Stones couldn't do that. They had sarcasm and cynicism and things to say but they couldn't do humor. It didn't work really. A lot of the lines were rehearsed. There was a little bit of chat between Lennon and Jagger that was vaguely amusing but by and large it was a bad show. The Who stole it. They played about ten times better than the Stones did on that. Jagger knew that. That's why he sat on it or whatever it was before it came out. It's now a collector's piece because it gives a kind of feeling of the end of the Sixties actually, even though it was a bit earlier than the end of the Sixties. I think it was the beginning of the end of the Sixties."

The program was not, as planned, sold to T.V. stations. Initially delayed because of the reasons Altham mentions, it instantly became a relic when Jones was sacked from the band the following year. A version of the film is now available on D.V.D.

Jagger and Richards have never publicly spoken of the dalliance between Jagger and Pallenberg and how the strains this must have injected into the four-way relationship—but particularly the relationship between Mick and Keith—were resolved. However, by late 1968, Jagger's betrayal of Richards had receded enough into history for the two of them along with Faithfull and Pallenberg to be friendly enough to all go on a trip to South America. Altham says, "It's always been one of those relationships that's had a certain love-hate relationship involved. Jagger and Richards. Daltrey and Townshend. There's always that kind of element within a really successful band where one almost wishes that [one] didn't need the other but they do and every time one makes a move sideways to do something else, of course they never come off as well as they do together."

No doubt a sense of solidarity was instilled in the two rebels' hearts when they were ejected from the Hotel Crillon in Lima, Peru, for insisting on wandering around bare-chested. Brian had experienced similar problems in January when a string of hotels in his holiday destination of Ceylon refused him admission, thinking his bright pink finery indicated poverty, eventually provoking him into slapping a handful of money down on a reception desk to prove otherwise. Such were the day-to-day hassles of being multi-colored individuals in a world still very much in monochrome.

The fact that the trip took place was ultimately highly felicitous. As Richards later explained of their stay in Brazil, "Went to a ranch and wrote 'Honky Tonk Women' because it was into a cowboy thing. All these spades are fantastic cowboys. Beautiful ponies and quarter horses. Miles from anywhere. Just like being in Arizona or something." It should be noted that although the public first heard the rock version of the song released on single as "Honky Tonk Women" and were then subsequently exposed to the country version titled "Country Honk" on *Let It Bleed*, the latter was not actually cooked up by the Stones as a lateral view of the song but actually far closer to the guitarist's original vision. Richards said, "We put that other version of 'Honky Tonk Women' on [*Let It Bleed*] because that's how the song was originally written, as a real Hank Williams/Jimmie Rodgers Thirties country song. And it got turned around to this other song by Mick Taylor, who got into a completely different feel, throwing it off the wall completely."

Richards would also later state that the vocal refrain and title line were an example of that classic rock 'n' roll tradition of a writer blocking in a part of the song with a dummy lyric which in the end came to feel so natural as to become irreplaceable. Or as he put it, "A lot of times you're fooling with what you consider to be just working titles or even working hooks, and then you realize there's nothing else that's going to slip in there and fit in the same way. So you're left with this fairly inane phrase." Inane title phrase or not, when it was released as a single in July 1969, "Honky Tonk Women" become an instantly iconic Stones song and would act as a superb harbinger to the *Let It Bleed* album. It also became a UK number one—the last chart-topper the band would have in Britain.

It must have been clear to Jagger and Richards by this point that the creative roll they had started with *Beggars Banquet* was continuing and that any friction or awkwardness engendered by the *Performance* affair was not going to adversely affect what had been one of the great composing partnerships in rock since around mid-1965. Asked if he spotted any fracture in Mick and Keith's friendship at this juncture, Olympic's George Chkiantz says, "I didn't see them sort of try to avoid each other. At all. I don't recall seeing any estrangement. Any recording session, there's going to be some tension, there's going to be some disagreements. The stuff is so close to anybody's emotions that you might well get [an argument] on purely musical levels. It could look like a family quarrel anyway. Although in fairness with the Stones that didn't happen that often."

In contrast to that pleasing aesthetic state of affairs were the continuing problems with Allen Klein. The Stones' exasperation with their manager's mysterious ways with their own money and his general tardiness erupted in a telex Jagger sent Klein in May 1969 about the cover design of their upcoming compilation album *Through The Past Darkly*, in which he said, "Your inefficiency is a drag. What the fuck did you do with all the photographs, not the press cuttings, the photographs? They were supposed to be delivered to Andy Warhol. We await your reply." The Stones found themselves frequently awaiting Klein's replies, about money, unpaid bills, and funds for various projects. Klein's lack of communication was exacerbated by the fact that telephoning him at his American office would in those days have cost a fortune that even the Rolling Stones balked at, and they were forced instead to resort to the method of cabling him their questions and complaints, a process whose cumbersomeness and lack of human contact kept it not far removed from Morse code.

Jagger's tone and language show a minimal respect for his manager, and demonstrate the way that the Stones' initial delight with Klein's business methods upon his appointment by Andrew Loog Oldham in mid-1966 had soured beyond redemption. Honeymoon periods between Klein and his clients were often inordinately blissful, what with his ability to make himself look like their champion. Klein—an accountant by training—once approached a US teen idol and asked him whether he would like to make a million dollars. "What do I have to do for it?" was the gist of the reply. "Nothing," responded Klein, explaining that if he were given authority by the artist to inspect his record company's accounts, he would uncover at least that amount in underpaid royalties. The condition was that Klein would receive a percentage for his pains. The teen idol, with nothing to lose from the deal, gave his authority, and within a brief period had his million dollars.

Fighting the artists' corner in a business operated by people who—then—had an equal contempt both for the product they were selling and for the artists who made it, and who therefore had no qualms about ripping them off, was inevitably going to impress rock stars. An additional draw was Klein's no-nonsense approach. Many rock artists came from humble backgrounds and had perfunctory educations. Consequently they were—especially in class-bound Britain—intimidated by the idea of questioning authority and bewildered by the intricacies of book-keeping. Klein was intimidated by nobody. Keith Altham recalls, "He did get results. I saw him operate once in the Hilton hotel with Jagger and Richards and we were all in the same room. He had three guys from A.T.V. downstairs waiting in the lobby who he kept waiting while he read a *Superman* comic on the loo or something and when they trooped into the room, Klein said, 'Right, which one of you gentlemen would like to talk on behalf of the other [two]?' And Mr Brown or whoever it was said, 'I think I can talk on behalf of my colleagues.' 'Right,' he said, 'I just need to know one thing from you Mr Brown. Can you sign your name on the bottom of a check on behalf of A.T.V.?' 'Well, no, I can't do that.' 'Goodbye, the audience is at an end.'"

It is safe to presume that a similar reluctance to take prisoners attended Klein's dealings with Decca Records, from whom he wrested large advances against record royalties for the Stones. The royalties were also renegotiated and were actually bigger than those of The Beatles—until Klein became *their* manager, too. He also secured from Decca a massive advance for the Stones to appear in a film adaptation of *Only Lovers Left Alive*, a novel by Dave Wallis in which teenagers take over the country. The project was announced in May 1966. It wasn't long afterwards that Altham remembers the band becoming disillusioned with Klein. Altham, "Klein went into Decca and said, 'I want a million dollars upfront for the film.' Then he asked Oldham where he wanted it to be paid and Oldham told him into this off-the-shelf company that the Stones had called Nanker And Phelge. After about a month, he thought he better check that the money was in the account and found out it wasn't in Nanker And Phelge in England at all but had gone into another account which Klein had formed called Nanker And Phelge Inc. in New York and it took them something like five years to get that money back, by which time Klein had had it invested in General Motors and copped all the interest. It was pretty much concerning this Nanker And Phelge thing that they did get rid of him."

In fact, it wasn't until May 1972 that the Stones were able to put out a statement that all claims between themselves and Allen Klein had been settled—a settlement rumored to have cost them just about every penny they had earned in the Sixties—but as Altham points out, "Once you've got contracts signed, it takes ages to actually completely free yourself of those kind of contractual obligations. It isn't just that 'We divorce thee, we divorce thee' routine. They couldn't free themselves of the music publishing contracts and things they'd signed with him for ages and ages, and of course he still owns large chunks of it." That the group were effectively forced to do business with a man with whom they already had no wish to interact must have been deeply depressing and upsetting.

The Rolling Stones rehearsed the songs that would appear on *Let It Bleed* in their rehearsal space in Bermondsey Street, Bermondsey, south-east London, a place they had alighted on after a lengthy search for a venue where neighbors would not complain about the noise they made. The rehearsal space was an old warehouse and consisted of two floors: ground floor and basement. The latter had a rather low ceiling, less than seven feet. The ground floor had a high ceiling and measured approximately 50 by 100 feet. It was on the ground floor that the Stones stored their equipment. In 1969, an eight-track Ampex tape machine was installed. When they weren't using the rehearsal space, they would allow other musicians to do so. In 1969 alone, it was visited by the Small Faces, the Spencer Davis Group, and Fat Mattress. The rehearsal space saw a lot of use during the several years that the Stones owned it. It now houses the theatrical magazine *The Stage*.

Some time in March, Brian Jones handed a letter to Jo Bergman, the Stones' long-term assistant, indicating his wish to use the band's resources to tape the musicians of the Moroccan tribe the Joujouka. The missive read, "Dear Jo, I need the following dates to do my recording thing in Morocco: 22–25 or 26 March. This is the only time I can get it done and I honestly believe I can get something really worthwhile from this venture for us. If this means I have to miss a session or two, I can dub my scenes on after, while vocals are being done or whatever. Incidentally, the Morocco thing is only part of my venture. I am confident I can come up with something really groovy. I will talk to you later about financing the thing, if that be possible. I don't need that much. Hope it happens! Love Brian."

It's almost certain that the rest of the Stones would have considered Jones's absence from some of the forthcoming sessions he mentions as more of a blessing than the nuisance his letter suggests. Kooper's previous comments give a flavor of the state of artistic decline that Jones had reached by now. It was a far cry from his glory days. Jones had two things that are considered a prerequisite for any pop idol but which by no means all pop idols have: incredible good looks and incredible talent. There is an argument for saying that Jones was the best-looking pop star of all time. In the early days, he looked like a sort of holy Beatle, his finely chiseled features sitting beneath an immaculate blond version of the mop-tops that adorned the Fab Four's heads. As the years progressed, his hairstyles became more impressive. Even in 1968—possibly the worse year of his life—he sported an immaculate haircut which framed in cascading drapes a face that now bore a pair of resplendent golden sideburns, even if a closer inspection would find his skin assuming an unhealthy pallor.

His first instrument had been the piano, on which he took lessons from ages six to fourteen. He also learned clarinet when young (which did his asthma no good). Jones, of course, initially co-pioneered the trademark intermeshing twin rhythm guitar Rolling Stones style with Richards. He was also a fine harmonica player. However, his interest in guitar waned during the mid-Sixties as he flitted from instrument to instrument, mastering each preposterously quickly, applying them as exotic sweeteners to a string of Stones songs, and then discarding them for the next musical challenge. Chkiantz says, "That was Stu's [Ian Stewart] comment, really. 'This guy is unbelievable, you wait and see. Anything that makes music, that guy'll pick up and in ten minutes he'll be getting music out of it' ... Brian was amazing in the sense that he could get music out of a keyring. If you put Brian in front of a completely new-fangled device, I'd put money on the fact that he'd get something out of it. Find a way of playing them." From 1966 to 1967, Jones can be heard playing the following instruments on Stones tracks: sitar ("Paint It Black", "Mother's Little Helper"), marimba ("Under My Thumb"), dulcimer ("Lady Jane"), recorder ("Ruby Tuesday"), and mellotron ("We Love You", "2000 Light Years From Home").

"Ruby Tuesday" is a song that some Stones insiders consider to be a Jones/Richards co-write. Certainly, Jagger himself has said, "I think that's a wonderful song. It's just a nice melody, really. And a lovely lyric. Neither of which I wrote." His generous admission sits at odds with the fact that the composition has always been credited to Jagger/Richards. However, the Stones' treatment of people who occupied the position of Third Most Important Stone—first Brian, then Mick Taylor, then Ronnie Wood—has always been characterized by a parsimonious attitude toward granting them songwriting credits and royalties. Perhaps this humiliation was a contribution to the reason for Jones's ever-increasing reluctance to take any constructive part in Stones sessions.

However, there were other, probably more important factors in his mental decline. One was the police harassment detailed earlier. Then there are the other reasons. "Brian was very talented and one should never forget that he founded the band with Ian Stewart," says Altham. "Without Brian Jones there would have been no Rolling Stones (or for that matter without Ian Stewart there would have been no Rolling Stones). The other guys joined their band and then Jagger and Richards became such a huge force within the band because they wrote the songs that the balance of power shifts and when the balance of power shifts, people become victims and they're injured. Brian was one of the casualties. But also he brought about his own problems by virtue of his drug problems and also his behavior. Right from the start, they found out he was taking a bit of extra money from [co-manager] Eric Easton because he told him he was the leader of the band or something. You don't do things like that in a group. That kind of thing didn't hold him in good stead when he probably needed the support perhaps he should have got. His behavior was pretty poor."

In addition to that power shift, Jones had lost the love of his life Anita Pallenberg to Keith Richards a couple of years before. As Altham points out, though, this was also partly due to his own intolerable actions, "I remember one of the first times I was round at Brian's place and Keith was coming out with Anita tucked under his arm *then* because she'd been beaten up by Brian. And I said, 'What's happened?' and he said something like, 'The little shit doesn't know how to treat his women' and took her away. And then he took her away a bit more permanently later on."

Nonetheless, one still can't help wondering why Jones did not do what so many people do when their personal lives are in turmoil: take solace in work and apply his professional skills to the best of his abilities. Altham says, "I think he was just out of it. He pretty much had the concentration of a mayfly anyway and [with] the drugs he really couldn't concentrate long enough to get anything together. And I think his confidence had been pretty much undermined during this period of time. I think Jagger and Richards got at him, to be honest. I don't think they were terribly kind to him during that period but Brian didn't exactly encourage kindness either. He was not exactly the best-behaved person in the world throughout the Stones' career, and when they saw a weakness, like a lot of guys in a gang, they used the weakness and I think it didn't help him any. He didn't really deserve the treatment he got—but then did he actually deserve much better, is the question."

All of which is not to say that the Joujouka excursion—which was approved by the Stones camp—was not an interesting idea. A field recording of the music of a Moroccan tribe, it was world music three decades before that idea became fashionable. It could also have provided some intriguing exotic ornamentation—in the best Brian Jones tradition—on a Stones album that, as it turned out, would have some of the most unusual decoration of their career thus far. Chkiantz recounts, "That was originally going to have the Rolling Stones dubbed all over it. Brian's bright idea was to make something out of it to make a contribution to the current Stones album. That was his initial idea. Now you've got to put this in context. Glyn [Johns] had gone over to

Morocco some months before and recorded the Gnawa, who were another tribe. I think Brian ran across them in Marrakech and I don't think Glyn went any further from home than Marrakech. He recorded the Gnawa and came back with a bunch of tapes and basically they were distorted, they weren't very good and in the end they couldn't really use much. I'd tape-oped on Glyn's kind of mix-down, look-through-it type sessions. The next thing that happened is that I suddenly found myself whisked off to Morocco. I think Glyn didn't really want to go to Morocco again or maybe he wasn't asked and Keith assigned this one to me, but I don't know how much Brian had asked for me. I know Keith was furious with me that day 'cos I got in late and [he] said, 'Another half-hour and I'd have had to send [for] "Irish" [Alan O'Duffy].' But I'd also expressed an interest because I'd always been interested in folk music and to some extent Arabic folk music. So I was pleased to go to Morocco and Glyn was very complimentary about the recordings that I'd actually done when we got them back and said I'd got far more out of exactly the same kit than he had. So then we started looking at it and the problem was we had some really good material but it wasn't at all obvious how this was going to act as a guitar solo or a solo in a Stones song. And also I personally thought it would be a totally criminal thing to do. So we had the tracks that have now wound up on side two of the [*Brian Jones Presents The Pipes Of Pan At Joujouka*] album, the flute ones. They held their own. And so we felt that could be put there. So the challenge was to do something with the other material, that we had to cook up an album side, and to me the challenge was to make it sufficiently sustain Brian's interest to stop him wanting to play guitar all over it, which to me personally, didn't seem like a good idea at all."

Ironically, Jones's original idea of using the Joujouka musicians as an exotic backdrop to a Rolling Stones track would reach fruition many years after his death with the track "Continental Drift" on the band's 1989 album *Steel Wheels*. Chkiantz says, "I suppose we might have done something like that but Brian got intrigued by the idea that the music should really stand on its own but didn't think an album of the pure material could hold its own in the wider market he had in mind unless we could do something pretty spectacular with what we'd got to do it. The result is what you see." Chkiantz is referring to the way the recordings were eventually turned into *Brian Jones Presents The Pipes Of Pan At Joujouka*, released belatedly in 1972 and one of the very few non-Stones albums ever issued on their own Rolling Stones Records label. (One of the others was another result of musical activities during the *Let It Bleed* recording period, *Jamming With Edward*.) At the time, Elektra Records expressed interest in releasing the album but the project foundered on the colossal indifference of Allen Klein who, as with so many things, repeatedly failed to respond to messages about it, something that rendered Jones distraught.

"At that time, it would never have been released if it hadn't got all the phasing all over it and all that, but for me it's a relatively successful depiction of what the trip to Morocco was like," says Chkiantz. "It was like a picture really, in a way. We kept the purest music pure. There isn't a sausage on [it]. Straight as it came off the tape, apart from just a bit of reverb at the end which I bitterly regret doing but it was only brought in about two seconds before it actually became obvious. That, if you like, preserved that music. I think he'd gone off the idea of blending it into the Stones or maybe he couldn't see how to do it." Did any of the other Stones express any interest in Brian's side-project? Chkiantz replies, "No. Don't think so. I mean, I am sure they stuck their head through the door and said, 'Very nice,' or something but they weren't asking for copies."

The Stones were extremely productive both before and during Brian's absence in Morocco.

From February 10 to March 31 1969, they recorded prolifically at Olympic Sound Studios, laying down not just many of the basic tracks of what would become *Let It Bleed* and the attendant "Honky Tonk Women" single but also several tracks that would become permanent offcuts or else would crop up on Stones albums several years down the line. Glyn Johns was back in the main engineer's role for the first sessions of this period.

Chkiantz explains the Stones' recording set-up at Olympic, "The way Glyn would tend to record—and I think we copied him to some extent—was like putting the musicians in horseboxes: we put a tall padded screen behind the guys with amplifiers, Bill and Keith. And we'd probably have put two behind Charlie. Sometimes we put him on a dais, sometimes we didn't. And then we put half-height screens between these sort of divisions and then half-height screens in front of them, which Charlie would have, too. I think we probably would have tended to put screens in front of Charlie but it might not have been that obvious that they were. They were really separation rather than trying to stop the sound out. In general, you want something to stop the bass drum going everywhere in the room. But to people observing it, especially if we didn't bother to actually screen the front of the drums, which is possible, or the screens had been moved aside and just left there, it might not have been so obvious that he'd been screened or it might have looked as though instead of just one screen vaguely in front of the bass ... it was just lying around. Charlie was screened by the shared ones. Because I don't think we tended to do that very closely. Certainly at Olympic we tended not to record in the manner that became popular, which is to put everybody in isolated booths. Glyn always adopted that particular approach. I should add that Olympic was one of the very few studios that actually had screens that were worth spitting at. Olympic screens did actually stop sound. Most other studios' screens that I ran into were pretty close to useless by comparison—they mainly tripped people up. There [were] normally screens behind [Charlie]. I think that was a psychological thing. I don't think the [back] screens made an awful lot of difference. I think they were more there to cut off the rest of the room from a psychological point of view." He continues, "The group would have been typically about a third of the way down the main studio, basically in a line facing the control-room window ... Probably they stood up mainly but chairs were around. There were stools around as well. And Keith playing acoustic of course would be sitting. Bill normally played standing up—but it depended how tired he'd got and how long it had been going on for."

O'Duffy says of Watts, "He'd have been on his own and multi-mic'ed. There might have been eight microphones on the kit. That was the way we did it at Olympic and that was the way really that Glyn did it. You'd rarely stick the drummer in a box. We were after a bigger sound than that."

Stones sessions differed from the legendarily enclosed, exclusive feel of Beatles sessions. "They had lots of friends," says O'Duffy. "Guys would call in. Girls as well would come by. It would be a party scene with the recordings from time to time. People would visit. Jimmy Miller's wife would be there. A lovely lady." Smith says, "Always a big sort of family atmosphere. People coming and going. Always a very social atmosphere. Lots of friends around, which was nice."

In addition to the band members, a Rolling Stones session would not be complete without the presence of Ian "Stu" Stewart, the no-nonsense, lantern-jawed man who had helped set up the group and then found himself deemed too ugly to be in a band by Andrew Loog Oldham. Stewart agreed to cast himself in a new role for the Stones. "Roadie, I suppose," says Chkiantz, "but I always thought 'roadie' was way inadequate. Stu was more their ambassador. He was far more than a head roadie and I think he loved the band for all his gripes. It was inconceivable to me that Stu would have gone anywhere else. Probably they must have happened but I don't recall a Stones session without Stu being there." Not that this prevented Stewart from harrumphing his way through many a Stones session as they drifted away from the blues-and-boogie image in which they had originally been molded. Chkiantz recalls, "I don't think he liked the direction they were going in particularly. What did he say about Charlie, 'He'd be far happier playing brushes behind Sarah Vaughan!'"

It is Stewart we have to thank for the knowledge about the Stones' amplifiers during the *Bleed* sessions. He revealed to *Beat Instrumental* just before the album's release that they used a mixture of 15-watt Watkins amps, an early Vox AC30 and some Fender models. Wyman played his Framus bass— an almost antiquated instrument that the band found his attachment to amusing—through a Hi-Watt amplifier. All were actually rather small amplifiers, especially considering the power of the band's sound.

By 1969, the Rolling Stones had drifted into the decadent recording modus operandi for which they would become famous and which can only occur when a group is part of the rock aristocracy: rich enough to waste time and money. "Stones sessions were pretty bizarre events," recalls Chkiantz. "Charlie would probably turn up within three-quarters of an hour of the official start time of the session. Most of the rest of them normally wouldn't turn up for two or three hours. So Charlie would have his drums set up and he'd play them and bash them around—drums need to be warmed up for a bit— and so on and we'd just be milling around or chatting. Then Bill would turn up. The thing would ramble together. The only way to make sure that all the Stones were in the same country at the same time and with a hope of getting them into the studio at the same time was to say, 'There is a session at two o'clock.' If it turned out that that meant that the last one would turn up four hours later, that was already a success. They'd got them all in the room. I don't understand how people like that live, not really." Naturally, the last to arrive would be Jagger and Richards, by now without question the songwriting and iconic nucleus on which the group depended.

Though such a procedure might seem incredibly wasteful to an outsider, the Stones were by no means a slovenly recording unit. As Smith puts it, "A different kind of discipline but much more relaxed. They're creating something quite different than a series of pop singles. They're creating more of an overall sound concept and I think they're very disciplined in their ways [but] they had the freedom to do it over a long period of time and I think that made the discipline have a different perspective to it. You had so much more time to get a drum sound. A whole day or two days. Or a guitar sound or a guitar solo. You had five weeks to do a vocal performance. That kind of thing. The discipline was more in achieving the best artistic performance and the best sound and then the combination of all the musicians. I think that's the discipline. It's something that I learned from them was the creativity—obviously with the budget allowing. A lot of artists wouldn't have that sort of budgetary time."

Did the engineers ever feel taken for granted by this decadent behavior? Chkiantz says, "I didn't but the studio certainly did. Keith [Grant] would get absolutely irate about it. Largely because maybe he had a film session that had overrun where he was trying to fit in film sessions or whatever. I think he just saw it as a waste of a facility when everybody was moseying around and he'd come along quite cheerfully and say, 'Where are they?' 'We've still got Mick and Keith to go.' He'd see a whole afternoon in which he would have done two adverts or a film or something. He got very annoyed with me for shifting session time where they'd have booked in from seven o'clock in the evening till the death and we'd have a night that actually went on till four or five in the morning, so instead of starting the next day's session at two—because that's what they'd booked—I'd leave a note for [studio admin person] Anna and slide it down to seven, or five. And he'd always get really annoyed at me and say, 'You can't do that.' And I'd say to him, 'Hang on a minute, you're making just as much money, because if we closed up at one o'clock in the morning—which we'd have wanted to do if were realistically going to get there and do anything at two—you in fact make more money from us working at night because you're getting the ramp-up that you do on night rates.' So, okay it's sort of intellectually irritating to see the studio blank, especially I'm sure when you feel can you fit somebody in. I think it was just different modes of living. Keith [Grant] was one of those people who said that he could not sleep beyond the dawn. He always woke up at dawn. So doing night work was an absolute nightmare for him. The rest of us were rather the opposite."

So irritated was Grant by the Stones' recording methods that when The Beatles decided to record the song "Baby You're A Rich Man" at Olympic in May 1967, he decided to try to impress them with the quality of the studio but not so much that they would want to record there again. Chkiantz remembers, "What he was out to do was to impress them that Olympic could outperform Abbey Road, but he didn't actually want them as clients and I said, 'What? Are you crazy or something?' He said, 'No. Look, we've already got the Stones, who come in and block-book the studio for loads of time so that other people don't get a look-in. All we need is for The Beatles to come up and take the rest of the time and those two to split the time between us and what I'm really worried about is what's going to happen to you guys? Because all of a sudden you're going to get into the habit of turning up two hours late for the session 'cos who's going to notice? And all the tautness and all the rest of it will just go.' Every so often Keith would feel we were getting slack or something and all of a sudden you were out on a nine o'clock [in the morning] ad session for a week, which was pretty fucking tough and none of us liked it. Keith felt it was a major thing if on a big orchestral session you weren't taking within quarter of an hour."

Nonetheless, the Stones were indulged by Grant to some extent. Chkiantz says, "There'd always be a huge thing where they were trying to get it for a cheaper rate, which we normally gave them." O'Duffy explains this, "I think really the Stones were responsible for a fantastic amount of the turnover in terms of cash that came into that studio at that time."

The tracks on which work was begun by the Rolling Stones during this period were: "French Gig", "Gimme Shelter", "Honky Tonk Women", "I Was Just A Country Boy", "Let It Bleed", "Love In Vain", "Pennies From Heaven", "Shine A Light", "Sister Morphine", and "You Got The Silver". Additionally, there may have been some other tracks recorded, although these are currently unverified: "Aladdin Story" and "Jimmy Miller Show." All were Jagger/Richards compositions except "Sister Morphine", which the pair co-wrote with Marianne Faithfull. In addition, overdub work was done on "You Can't Always Get What You Want".

Even the unobservant will have instantly noticed that some of these tracks have titles that bear no relation to anything officially released by the band. The Stones always recorded more tracks than a 40-minute vinyl L.P. could accommodate, something proved by the abundance of the 1972 double album *Exile On Main Street* (not, contrary to popular mythology, recorded in one go in Keith Richards's basement but a selection of tracks from several different years) and 1981's *Tattoo You* (a collection of even more wildly varying vintages). As Jagger told Roy Carr in 1977, the Stones could easily have released two albums per year, even if one of those albums would be not quite as good as the other. It never happened, but the closest it ever came to happening was in fact 1969. In June of that year, the Stones—clearly heady with their productivity—announced that they would be releasing two long-players in '69, one in September, the second in December. The first was scheduled to be titled *Sticky Fingers*.

"You Got The Silver"—originally called "You Got Some Silver Now"—was a lovely song of devotion, almost certainly written by Keith alone and therefore almost certainly about Anita Pallenberg. Marianne Faithfull has recalled Keith debuting it for a select audience of four sitting on the four-poster bed of art dealer Robert Fraser, their co-defendant in the 1967 drug trial. "Keith's method is to take the germ of a song and nag at it, all the while keeping it to himself," she wrote in her autobiography. "It stays in his head until it's finished. And then out of the blue, he'll drop it on you. A dazzling thing to do." Perhaps it's too glib to read things into songs when one knows about some of the circumstances of their writer's private life at the time, but the quasi-worship underpinning the song perhaps gives an indication of why

Richards was able to forgive Pallenberg her transgression. Its vulnerability is certainly a refreshing counterpoint to the macho mentality of so many Stones songs.

Though Keith probably wrote it and though it was his pleasantly reedy voice that was ultimately to be heard singing it on the finished album, it would seem that originally Jagger was intending to do the song's lead vocals. A version with a Mick vocal exists. It is an interesting alternate take, less ornate than the *Bleed* one and with a slightly muffled quality (although the latter could be merely down to the fact that it was not a master recording and full EQing was not necessary). Apart from a slightly drawled character, Jagger's delivery is actually very similar to the familiar Richards one: he accentuates the same phrases and leaps into the same emotiveness at the same junctures as does Keith. The Jagger vocal seems to be on a different backing track.

"You Got The Silver" saw some of the only contributions to the album by Brian Jones, who played autoharp. Chkiantz recalls, "There's some high-up stuff on that. There was some high guitar stuff which he did with car keys, harmonics and stuff." Asked if it would be too cruel to suggest this was a contrived way for the increasingly incapable and sidelined Jones to get on to the recording, Chkiantz says, "No. I'd probably have thought that many years ago, but you've got to accept the fact that he must have been doing that. Brian clearly had been sidelined a long, long time before. Mick and Keith would not argue if Brian really wanted to do something or try something or whatever. They'd kind of tend to let it go. I don't know how much in the end they did that thinking, 'We can always wipe it.' There must have been a bit of both. There must have been some part of them that desperately wanted what they knew Brian could play. And was desperately at the same time in despair with what he actually produced and thinking, 'What the hell do we do about this?'" It was this kind of desperation on the part of Jones that indicated just how far his capabilities and musical vision had deteriorated. Chkiantz says of Jones's ability to master any instrument, "That never left him. In so far as his coordination would hold together, he could do it. But I think it was a different story of trying to find himself a place to fit in with the track, with the band going in a musical direction he probably didn't really like. He'd just say, 'Oh, I just want to do this little thing, it'll just add a little bit to the edge of this' and so on and so forth and that's so unlike a lead player especially [who'll usually say], 'Blam, I'll take over, thank you.' You do see players do this kind of thing. There have been other players who have sort of tried to hide themselves in the murk."

Chkiantz has a feeling that it was "You Got The Silver" that the Stones were recording when Jimmy Miller's—to him—over-fussy production style caused Richards to bleed. "The format very frequently and on this occasion was, the group having finally sort of coalesced in the studio, Charlie having warmed up his drums, variously people would go down, start playing, come back, and one of the parts of that would be that Keith would go down and start playing. The minute Keith started playing, that's when things started to get a bit more serious and [we'd] listen to what Keith was playing. Maybe Charlie would then go down and they'd start fitting in around it. That would be the key for serious [work]. So if you think about it, Keith would have been playing for longer than anybody else. The minute they started playing in a formalized sort of way then Keith is going to be playing until it's finished, pretty much. And it was during this time that we got into this thing that Jimmy was worried about the snare sound, which was perfectly typical and had happened loads and loads of times before. You carry along with it and you do what you can but beyond a certain point you're not even sure that you're getting anywhere … This was where Jimmy was doing a number about getting the drum sound completely right. The geometry of it is that there's a group out in the studio. Keith is in the isolation booth, which was a kind of room, the little annex at the end of the control room. You walked through this booth, it had two fridge [cooler] doors, then you got into a little lobby a few steps up to the level of the desk of studio one. This drum-sound thing was going on for quite some time. Keith was laying down the acoustic rhythm basis of the track. He came up while Jimmy was going on about something and tapped me on the shoulder and said, 'Look, can we get this together quickly please because I really want to get this track down tonight because I think it's right and my hands are beginning to bleed and I really can't play it that many more times.'" Chkiantz glanced down at the guitarist's hands to find them streaked with red. "Obviously I was frightened," he says. "I had no idea that something like that was happening and so I said, 'Sure, I'll do what I can.' When Jimmy started doing the drum thing again, I said to him, 'Keith wants to get it done now because his hands are beginning to go.' So all of a sudden we stopped talking about the drum sound and started going for takes and did make it fairly soon afterwards. What shocked me was—I don't know whether it was after the master take or during a break—but I went through the vocal booth on my way to the kitchen to get a coffee or tea or water or whatever—and I could see that there was blood streaming from the neck of his guitar, which must have been agonizing for him. I was really quite surprised how Keith—who's quite ferocious; I've seen him take people to pieces in nice little strips—how gentle and kind he was about something which must hurt him physically far more than somebody running into the back of his Bentley did."

The master take of "You Got The Silver" was completed on February 17 and may have only been the third take of the track.

February 23 to the 25 saw the band making their first attempts at a song they were still calling "Give Me Some Shelter". Released eventually as "Gimme Shelter" (although some pressings have rendered the first word as "Gimmie"), it was a song of fear and foreboding, talking of storms and streets of fire threatening the narrator's life. It would be the opening track of the album and to this day is in many people's opinion the band's masterpiece. In a poll of critics and musicians in 2001, the track emerged as the number one Jagger/Richards song of all time. Meanwhile, noted American rock critic Greil Marcus said of the song in 1978, "May well be the greatest single rock and roll performance."

The song would seem to have been written by Richards alone. This is rather appropriate if we are to accept the speculation by Faithfull that the desperate, even apocalyptic imagery of its lyric was Richards's way of expressing his anguish over what Jagger and Pallenberg had done to his trust and self-confidence during the filming of *Performance*. Richards wrote the song in Robert Fraser's flat, where he and Pallenberg were then living. "It was a very gray afternoon," Richards later told *Uncut* magazine. "It was basically just like chord structure at first. It just keeps going up and down. It's a strange sort of scale. Although actually to me there was always more of a feeling to that song than actually musically how it's played. It's really more of a spirit in a way. After all, storms are storms."

Chkiantz, when asked if it seemed destined for such status at the time says, "I suppose to a degree they did. It was a special track."

To a degree, there was no way of knowing if a Stones track would transpire to be an extravaganza. As O'Duffy explains, the Stones would tend to work hand to mouth, "I worked subsequently with Paul McCartney and he arrived with the entire lyrics for an entire album which I made with him called *Venus And Mars*. Paul had the lyrics written out and photocopied and he gave me a copy of every word that's going to be in this next album, 'And the album's going to be called *Venus And Mars*, here you are.' Now I don't think that the Stones worked in that manner at all. I'm sure that Keith, Brian, Mick had an idea of the songs they were going to try and put together but there wasn't a clearly defined map for the production."

"The Triumph amplifiers were the key to 'Gimme Shelter'." says Chkiantz. He is referring to the fact that the Stones had recently acquired some amplifiers manufactured by the company Triumph (he suspects Ian Stewart had got them on trial) and that Richards had discovered an interesting quirk about their sonic qualities. Chkiantz says, "They had these lights along the top. They were transistorized actually—which was kind of not usual for the Stones. What they discovered was that these amps would produce this amazing crunch once they'd just got to a certain stage of overheating, just before they'd turn themselves off or blew up or something, and you can tell by the dimness of the lights. As the lights dimmed—you had to have them at just exactly the right volume and they had had to be going like that for just the right amount of time—then suddenly the sound out of them would produce this extraordinary sound, the core to that track. So we had great fun. 'We need to bash the amps around a bit.'"

This kind of lateral thinking characterized Richards's working practices at the time. On *Beggars Banquet*, Richards had come up with ingenious uses for portable tape recorders and the extraordinary noise they generated when the batteries were partially flat. Similar outside-the-envelope thinking attended the recording of "Gimme Shelter". Chkiantz continues, "Keith was determined that they had to be at this exact point in time, which was probably a temperature thing which was after so many hours of this. And then after that, they had to be allowed to cool down for a bit and then reheated up to get them at their sweet spot. They're terrible amplifiers otherwise. This is like Phil Spector using that mad studio in California which had the echo chamber that sounded wonderful and nothing else."

The finished track would ultimately be lacerated with colossal-sounding blasts of mouth harp. This saw some more ingenuity based around getting things to sound like they weren't supposed to sound. Chkiantz says, "The harp's 'magic ingredient' was using the distortion caused by overdriving an old Dynacord tape loop machine, then through other devices like limiters, etc. It also had to be set just right, but we were lucky that time."

All of this, of course, was hugely time consuming, with recording takes dependent not just on the presence of the personnel but on waiting around for optimum conditions. How did the other Stones react to this process? Chkiantz says, "Charlie was Charlie and just sort of did what he was asked to basically. Bill much the same I think. Everybody who was in that band must have known which way their bread was buttered … however much they might disagree on their personal opinions, so Bill and Charlie especially would maybe go along with decisions that they didn't really understand or even necessarily agree with. That was the way the band worked. It wasn't a bad ship. Stu would grumble forever. He didn't really like Nicky Hopkins playing piano. He didn't really like the direction the band was going in. He used to ask me, 'Do you really like that?' I'd say, 'Yeah, I like it.' 'Hmm.' Then he'd retire back and go and listen to his jazz night things. I don't think the others were exactly cowed but my interpretation would be they'd accepted the formula. They were in the right band for them. They'd outlasted everybody else by then and the machine was still working. They were still making money. In fact, they were probably making more money. I think it went on much later where Bill really got dissatisfied. Sure, Bill was up to his own things, he liked doing his own production stuff with The End." Though Jagger played no other instruments than harmonica/mouth harp and basic guitar at this point in his life, he wasn't in the same position as were the rhythm section of twiddling his thumbs while things like this went on. "Mick was a loudmouth," says Chkiantz. "Mick was the producer cum co-producer."

In any event, a comment made to *Beat Instrumental* by Ian Stewart about the making of *Let It Bleed* indicates that by this point, an all-for-one, one-for-all attitude was informing Stones sessions. "All the group were really enthusiastic about making it. Sometimes in the past, if one of the group wasn't needed at a particular session, he wouldn't come. On this one, everyone was there nearly all the time, even on the mixing sessions."

Ian Stewart was of course the band's original pianist and a man who would still be called upon to contribute backing tracks when friends like Jack Nitzsche and Nicky Hopkins weren't around. However, it was Nicky Hopkins providing piano on "Gimme Shelter". Hopkins—who had first worked with the Stones on *Between The Buttons*—was well on his way to becoming a name synonymous with the Stones, so much so that some have recalled him expressing bewilderment at the fact that the band did not ask him to join their ranks as a permanent member. However, the Stones were only one plank of the rock aristocracy for whom Hopkins provided his sterling keyboard services. The Beatles had used him on the "Hey Jude" B-side "Revolution", while he had long been a favored session man of producer Shel Talmy and thus ended up on classic records by The Who, The Creation, and The Kinks. (It's rumored that The Kinks' song "Session Man"—on which he played harpsichord—is actually about him.)

That Hopkins should come to enjoy this prominence and respect was the culmination of a story that could have ended in tragedy—and perhaps did, for he died young— aged fifty—in 1994. "We always had to be really careful about Nicky," recalls Chkiantz of his earliest Stones sessions. "They'd just fucking taken away most of his insides. He'd had twenty-five or thirty major operations in eighteen months. Much later, Andy [Johns] told me that one day he'd seen him in a swimming pool [and] he just couldn't believe it. It was kind of like half his body wasn't there. There was this gap. The story I heard was that Nicky had these absolutely appalling operations and he was told in no uncertain terms that he wasn't to play the piano or to get excited or to do anything. Glyn knew Nicky from before and kind of thought, 'Well maybe we can get him out to play. What's the difference between sitting at home bored stiff and doing something that you actually like to do?' The doctors weren't in the least bit keen, but Nicky was because he wanted to play. Suddenly they just heard however many years it was that he'd been having operations and being ill and recuperating—it just sort of poured out of him. It was just unreal and unbelievable. From then on we had this kind of thing that Nicky was not to be made to wait outside the studio. He had to wait in the control room where it was warm until his cab turned up. It wasn't the slightest problem because we all liked him. Nicky was bent-shouldered, quite gray—his complexion was gray—he did

The Stones in rehearsal at London's Saville Theatre, December 14, 1969: left to right, Mick Taylor,
Charlie Watts, Mick Jagger, Keith Richards, and Bill Wyman.

Mick Jagger

All the pictures of The
Rolling Stones on this
page and opposite were
taken October 27, 1969
at a press conference
held at the Beverly
Wilshire Hotel, Los
Angeles, prior to their
American tour.

Keith Richards

Bill Wyman

Charlie Watts

*Guitarist Brian Jones,
when he was still firmly
ensconsed as a member
of the Rolling Stones,
attending the Monterey
International Pop Festival
in California, July 1967.*

*Jones' replacement Mick
Taylor, also taken at the
Beverly Wilshire press
conference in 1969.*

A rare studio shot of Keith, Mick, and singer Bonnie Bramlett (who never appeared on the LP) at Elektra
Studios, LA, October 1969

n the Elektra playback room, Keith and Mick with producers Jimmy Miller and Glyn Johns.

The Stones in the Park—the legendary Hyde Park concert in London, July 5, 1969.

Memorable for all the wrong reasons—the band at Altamont Speedway, Livermore, California on December 6, 1969.

The Stones lined up for a photo call in Hyde Park on June 13, 1969 when they announced guitarist Mick Taylor (2nd left) would be the replacement for Brian Jones.

Mick and Keith get their ya-yas out during a September Danish date on their 1970 European trek.

not look healthy at all but he was a lovely guy. We all loved him dearly. He was huge fun."

A couple of intriguing early versions of "Gimme Shelter" have leaked out. One of them has tinkly piano bits in the opening bars as well as the darker piano tones familiar from the officially released version. Jagger and Richards sing the lead vocal together. The vocal melody line sounds slightly mechanical and underdeveloped, with the two not having found all the nuances and optimum stresses yet. On the mouth-harp interjections, Mick's gulping and huffing for air is picked up by the harp mic. Another, presumably later, version has bass bobbing prominently in the opening bars. The rest of the backing sounds like it is the take of the familiar version, but Jagger's vocal track is different. The choruses ("War, children," etc.) are sung by all-male voices and in a style rather akin to a football-ground chant. The mouth-harp interjections are lower down in the mix and therefore not as dramatic and ominous as on the *Bleed* version. Jagger sings the "rape, murder" line that would be sung by female vocalist Merry Clayton on the final versions. Altogether, the track is only really subtly different from the one the world knows but is nothing like as stunning as that one, the apocalyptic, almost fearful air not quite there and in fact the ambience boasting an inappropriate semi-defiance.

March 9 saw the group tackle the song that Keith had begun to cook up in South America, "Honky Tonk Women". (The same day may have seen their first attempt at the track "Let It Bleed", then called "If You Need Someone".) The bluesy tones of "Honky Tonk Women" were one musical direction at least that Ian Stewart could agree with, and it was he who provided piano accompaniment—even if that accompaniment, like many ornamental elements of the song, would ultimately be lost in a mix that was rather peculiar. That mix though was well into the future: "Honky Tonk Women" was a track the band would keep coming back to.

The same perfectionism marked the development of "Midnight Rambler", though for different reasons. Whereas the basic track of "Honky Tonk Women" would be recorded again and again, it was the instrumental passages of "Midnight Rambler" that would be worked and reworked obsessively following a fairly easy recording of the basic track. The band may have first tackled "Midnight Rambler" on March 9 or 10 but definitely recorded a version on either March 10 or 11.

"I did a lot of work on that," says Smith. "One of my strongest memories is the guitar solo. We spent a whole week doing the guitar solo, which was all done in one take. So it would happen night after night. Just Keith would come in the studio with Jimmy and we'd be doing the 'Midnight Rambler' guitar solo and if that atmosphere wasn't right or the vibe wasn't right for that night, we'd jack it and come back another night. I think it took about five nights to get the final take. Once again, we're talking about erasing every performance and no synchronization there of loading it onto a hard disk or something and then flying different versions back in like you can today. You're talking about just losing it. That was very memorable actually. It went through a lot of changes. It's quite a substantial guitar piece on there and never a boring moment to work on that. It was good. At that point when we got to the solo, it just bound the whole track together. It was a crucial part of the track. It's just there were days where it just never happened. There were some nights Keith just couldn't get it together at all. You just have to be in the right mood, you just have to have the right kind of atmosphere. And I think the night that it actually happened—obviously one rehearses all the stuff at home and goes over ideas and you're kind of faced with the track and you're in the cold studio environment again—it just kind of happened and it was just absolutely brilliant. I can't remember actually if we dropped in but I think in a lot of cases it was just a complete performance. Dropping in halfway through a track wasn't that sophisticated technically then. You'd have a huge sound bump if you dropped in unless there was an actual gap in the sound."

As for Jagger's powerful and menacing singing, Smith says, "Always impressed by his vocal performance. The energy. That magnetism. That really got me." "The interesting thing about Mick Jagger is that Mick Jagger doesn't have the greatest voice in the world," says Alan O'Duffy. "He doesn't have the greatest set of larynx. He doesn't have the greatest, if you like, vocal timbre. But, my God, is he a brilliant singer. He is a phenomenal singer and his sense of rhythm—his rhythmic feel, his interpretation of a lyric in a rhythmic way, his tunefulness, and so on—is fantastic. And his charisma, listening to him. Forget the way he looks, which is brilliant, he makes a fantastic contribution to humanity by his singing. Only guys like me [have] had the privilege of hearing Mick Jagger singing without the backing track and you just hear the guy going for it and he is fantastic. He drives the band."

March 15 saw the Stones doing more work on "Gimme Shelter". That same day occasioned the visit to Olympic Sound Studios of members of the London Bach Choir, whose unlikely presence had been requested to provide decoration to "You Can't Always Get What You Want". The choir is comprised of adults, not children as has sometimes been reported. However, Chkiantz remembers a certain star-struck quality among the choir members that one would associate with teenagers or people even younger. "It was really weird: fifty had been booked and sixty turned up." He also adds, "They came with milk bottles, with a crate of milk, like in primary school!"

Stones friend Jack Nitzsche had prepared a choral arrangement for the choir. Chkiantz recalls a real contrast of cultures at the session. "That was hilarious," he says. "Totally strange. The hard rockers one end swathed in billowing smoke in the control room and then fifty feet of no man's land with the choir at the other. The back end of Olympic was where we did choirs. There was a sort of arch and the choir needed to be done between the arch and the screen because it was a bit 'liver,' there was better sustain. So you had them all organized, even on rostrums I think. We got this sound. It was just amazing. But every time something needed changing, a lone brave person was detailed to go across no man's land and talk to the arranger. It really was like they almost needed white flags."

It would seem that initially the choir was just brought in to add the soaring backing harmonies on the track to build its drama, and that their unaccompanied recitation of the chorus that begins the familiar version was an accident.

Chkiantz recalls, "We'd done it, there was some talk of double-tracking and then we thought, 'No,' and [Mick] said, 'I really wish we could get them to do it a cappella (he didn't use that term) without the track.' He didn't know how to ask them. In the meanwhile we had cut the speakers. When we turned round, took the cut button off to try and introduce them to the idea, they were already doing it. They just got bored so they just started doing it. At this point, Mick was hastily putting down a cigarette. Made his way across no man's land with great enthusiasm. And so we recorded that bit too."

The result was not only pretty novel but, as Chkiantz observes, "I don't think anybody else [in rock] had used a full choir at that stage." Such is the attractiveness of the sound of the choir—and the track overall—that the logic of having it on the song is never really addressed. What is its significance? Chkiantz expresses the lack of concern of most over the issue when he shrugs, "Just sounds like a good thing to put on. Albums of the time. 'Oh we're going to get some strings in.' It started off we'd get some brass players who knew how to play, then you start getting sections in and you got odd orchestral sections which put a bit of orchestral color into the thing and you got that all over the place. I don't know whose idea it was but the choir certainly was a good idea. It certainly worked. It might have just been a kind of novelty thing. I don't know. I just think somebody sort of said, 'Hey, you know what would sound good on that?'" Al Kooper observes, "It made no sense whatsoever but it was terrific. Probably just for that reason. It was quite an original thing to do." O'Duffy says, "There was a thing with the

Stones where anything goes. You'd think, 'Hey, great.' They weren't afraid to experiment and look at new avenues of fulfilling their musical dream."

Though a choral section was something utterly un-rock 'n' roll, and though the Stones would occasionally display such baroque tendencies (e.g. strings on "Moonlight Mile" and "Angie"), from what Chkiantz says this is something that didn't come as naturally to them as it might, for instance, to The Beatles. "The minute their music became more orchestral in nature or in scope, I think they would get terribly worried and say, 'Well, no we're just a rock 'n' roll band really,'" he observes. "They find their way into that thing and slightly think they ought to do a real blues track and it all gets all kind of out of hand." Nonetheless, before the album was completed, "You Can't Always Get What You Want" would become even more ornate.

the honky tonk blues

March 23 saw the band work on a mid-tempo track (with piano) that was referred to on the tape ledgers as "I Was Just A Country Boy". It has no vocal but is clearly not an instrumental but a backing track for an unreleased song. As ever with such tracks, it's difficult to gauge what kind of quality it would have achieved had a vocal track been applied.

From March 24 to 27, the group worked on "Love In Vain". It was the only track on the finished album that would feature a contribution by session man Ry Cooder. Cooder's presence at the sessions would lead to one of the more contentious episodes of the Stones' recording career.

"Love In Vain" was written by Robert Johnson, a mythic figure in blues, of whom then no picture was known to exist. Johnson was born illegitimately in 1911 in Missouri. He and his mother lived an itinerant lifestyle that saw Johnson work on plantation cotton fields while still a young boy. He married at the age of 17, but his wife died in childbirth when the two had only been married just over a year. It was the only period of stability in Johnson's life, and his itinerant behavior resumed as a consequence of the tragedy. Johnson began pursuing a musical career, specializing in bottleneck guitar, and would seem to have thrown himself into practice after his wife's death. His technique leapt in astonishing increments, with him graduating from a mediocre to a great guitarist in a six-month span, so much so that a myth grew up to explain it.

Johnson, it was claimed—often by fellow musicians envious of his gifts and his rapid development—had gone down to the crossroads at Highways 61 and 49 in Clarksdale, Missouri (such intersections being traditionally regarded as places of evil-doing in American black country communities), where he made a deal with the Devil himself: his soul for technique. It was a leap in logic that had been helped by frequent references to the Devil in his often anguished songs ("Hellhound On My Trail", "Me And The Devil Blues"), plus the song "Crossroads Blues".

In 1936, this increased proficiency gained him a deal with Don Law's American Record Company whereby he would receive up to $15 for each song he recorded for them. Johnson laid down 17 songs (plus alternate takes) in a three-day period in a hotel room, some of them his own compositions, some adaptations of others. Johnson recorded 12 more songs the following year on two consecutive days at the Brunswick Records Building in Dallas, Texas. They would be his last recordings.

One of only two pictures that have since emerged of Johnson shows him to be a rather dapper figure: despite his poverty, he wears an immaculate pin-striped suit, carefully knotted tie, pocket handkerchief and a hat at a jaunty angle. Johnson was clearly something of a ladies' man, and this may have proved his undoing. In August 1938, he died after going into convulsions after drinking from an open whisky bottle on a table. It is thought that he was poisoned by a man whose wife he had come on to. Typically of his myth-laden life, no one is sure of his last resting place: two sites in Mississippi purport to be his grave.

The catalogs of major Sixties rock bands with their roots in blues are peppered with the works of Robert Johnson, "Come On In My Kitchen", "From Four Till Late", "Hellhound On My Trail", "Stop Breakin' Down Blues", "I'm A Steady Rollin' Man", "Terraplane Blues", "Cross Road Blues" (aka "Crossroad"), "If I Had Possession Over Judgment Day", and "Rambling On My Mind" amongst them. In addition to the Rolling Stones, those who have covered his material include such luminaries as Canned Heat, Eric Clapton, Cream, Bob Dylan, Fleetwood Mac, Led Zeppelin, Lynyrd Skynyrd, Status Quo, and the Steve Miller Band.

Up until the late Sixties, it had been thought that Johnson had left behind no bigger a canon than the 16 recordings contained on the album *King Of The Delta Blues Singers*. Then, miraculously, another cache of his recorded songs turned up, doubling his catalog. Initially, they only appeared on bootleg, the new medium in rock that had been started by the illicit release of the recordings Bob Dylan and the band had made in Woodstock in 1967 during Dylan's temporary disappearance from public life. Though Jagger and Richards had moved on from being the 12-bar purist blues fanatics of their early days, Johnson's music still had a big emotional and aesthetic pull for them. They decided to cover one of these newly found Johnson songs. Richards later said, "'Love In Vain' was such a beautiful song. Mick and I both loved it." In reference to a pioneering country-rock musician he had recently befriended, he continued, "At the time I was working and playing around with Gram Parsons, and I started searching around for a different way to present it, because if we were going to record it there was no point in trying to copy the Robert Johnson style or ways and styles. We took it a little bit more country, a little bit more formalized, and Mick felt comfortable with that."

Ry Cooder's contribution to the version of "Love In Vain" heard on *Let It Bleed* was mandolin. Cooder was at the time a prolific session musician, and not yet the solo recording artist he would become in the Seventies. He would appear on recordings by Paul Revere and The Raiders, Taj Mahal, Randy Newman, Little Feat, and Captain Beefheart, playing a variety of styles on a variety of string instruments. He was recruited by Jack Nitzsche to play on the soundtrack to Jagger's movie *Performance*. The connection perhaps inevitably led the Stones—still lacking that vital fifth member—to recruit his services. Richards later said, "We said, 'Do you want to come along and play?' The first thing Mick wanted was to re-cut 'Sister Morphine' with the Stones, which is what we got together. He's also playing mandolin on 'Love in Vain' … He played beautifully, man."

"Sister Morphine" had started in 1968 as a collaboration between Faithfull and Jagger. Faithfull later recalled Jagger having the melody line for several months and not knowing what to do with it. She presented him with a tale of an injured man gaining sweet release from his pain via the titular drug. Faithfull has suggested—though doesn't seem sure—that the line the "pure white sheets stain red" and the very concept of the song may have originated with the Jagger/Richards/Faithfull/Pallenberg foursome's Latin America travels that year. The pregnant Pallenberg had begun bleeding and persuaded a doctor to give her a shot of morphine, much to the envy of the smack-dabbling Richards and Faithfull. Faithfull has also suggested that the Velvet Underground's recent depictions of junkie squalor were an influence on the lyric, as well as the fact that she felt that this kind of lyric would appeal to Jagger and Richards. Faithfull's own version appeared as a single in February 1969 but was hastily withdrawn after only days when Decca top brass panicked about its content.

Work was done on the Stones' remake of "Sister Morphine" on March 22, 28, 30, and 31, with Cooder playing slide. (There is another unverified version from 1968.) One version featured Hopkins on piano, another was done without piano. "I did the basic on that one," recalls Chkiantz. "Strange night, that. The color of the air was very oppressive and thunder-stormy." Did that feed into the recording process? Chkiantz says, "Probably. Things do, you know." The final version was a powerful and haunting performance and would have made a great inclusion on the album. Instead it was held over and would only materialize on the album that would be called *Sticky Fingers*, released in 1971.

March 31st may also have seen the Stones attempt "Get A Line On You", a song that would take even longer to appear, ending up—retitled "Shine A Light"—on 1972's *Exile On Main Street*. However this early version is unverified.

There was then a hiatus in the recording of the album, lasting until April 17. Bill Wyman spent his time productively. He was the manager of a psychedelic pop band called The End. March 4, April 3, and April 15 saw The End recording sessions at Olympic with Wyman sitting in the producer's chair. "I think he quietly got what he wanted or what he could, which is what a producer does," says Chkiantz of Wyman. "I did quite a lot of those sessions and I enjoyed them. I liked Bill. Even went to his house a couple of times."

In April, Pallenberg was shooting *Umano Non Umano!* (*Human, Not Human!*) in Rome, Italy. The film would feature a couple of Stones-related sections, one of which featured Jagger miming to the track of "Street Fighting Man", the other featuring Richards playing on a Moog synthesizer. Also in April, Jagger and Richards took a month-long holiday in the hill town of Positano, Italy. They came up with some powerful new songs there: "Midnight Rambler"—a song abut a menacing figure with allusions to the mass murderer known as the Boston Strangler—and "Monkey Man". "That's a song Keith and I really wrote together," Jagger later recalled of "Midnight Rambler". "Why we should write such a dark song in this beautiful, sunny place, I really don't know. We wrote everything there—the tempo changes, everything. And I'm playing the harmonica in these little cafés, and there's Keith with the guitar."

Such a gap in a Stones album session at this point was not unusual. As O'Duffy explains, "I don't think they particularly had a plan called 'We're now going to make *Beggars Banquet* album.' There wasn't a concept like that. I think it was more like, 'Well let's go in and see what happens. Let's have a bit of fun. Let's get some backing tracks down. Let's see what we can do.' That was more the idea. And then the record evolved. It was continuous." Chkiantz elaborates, "People like the Stones, the sessions aren't as preset in blocks. The whole story with a band like the Stones is that there's an enormous amount of difficulty in finding them all in the same country at the same time and even more difficulty in persuading them all to come to the same place at the same time, so for all the intentionally efficient logistics, Mick may well say, 'Oh yeah, we started that then and we did the recording until then,' but actually they were in and out of the studios quite often. Things were done very non-linearly. Tracks would be put down, brought out to put an overdub on because somebody had turned up. It might work, it might not. It might get scrapped, it might get redone. For a band like the Stones, there was a continuum of a recording process where sessions were interspersed between gigs and what-have-you and ideas and times off. If they were around and felt like they ought to get on with something, they'd book some sessions in anyway and then they'd find out what they'd got."

"The reason it took so long was that it was simply a case of taking studio time when it was available," Ian Stewart would later say of the recording of *Let It Bleed*. "They've always got plenty of songs written, so it's not a problem waiting for that."

Clearly, considering the profusion of recording studios in London, so much did the Stones think of Olympic that at this point in time they could not countenance using any other studio in their home country if Olympic wasn't available and therefore were prepared to wait. They were also prepared, at least on one occasion, to countenance using Olympic's studio 2 if the main one was not at their disposal. On April 17, when the Stones reconvened at Olympic, it was in studio 2 that they began work on a new song that initially was given the title "Positano Grande" after Mick and Keith's recent holiday destination. Eventually, it would be titled "Monkey Man".

Dripping with playfulness and decadence (summed up by the line "All my friends are junkies/Well that's not really true"), like many tracks on the album its lyrics seemed to be a two-fingered salute to the band's elderly detractors (summed up by the immortal couplet "I hope we're not too messianic/Or a trifle too satanic"). Despite its grubby ambience, its arrangement was rather glossy. This may have been because George Chkiantz found himself having to give way in the engineer's chair to the more experienced, and in some ways more mainstream, Vic Smith.

Though a perfectly good recording room, studio 2 lacked the grandness of Olympic's main studio. "It's a small room," explains Chkiantz. "Its capacity was probably eighteen to twenty musicians, as opposed to studio 1 which was about seventy. [The ceiling] was quite high for a room of its size but you weren't in a well. I guess the whole studio 2 thing was about forty foot into the anteroom into the control room and the width would have been twenty-five, I suppose."

Recording the basic track of "Monkey Man" in studio 2 was not going well on the April 17. Chkiantz recalls, "The small studio ... was simply no good for the Stones really. It really wasn't a good idea. The Stones were like too big to go into number 2. I was very much the person who looked after, who got number 2 working, but I could not apparently [that day]. And the reason I found it very difficult [was that] number 2 was okay as long as you turned a blind eye to some of the things which really were not good in there—but I couldn't persuade the collective might of all of them to turn that blind eye. I knew the results that I was going to deliver would be okay, 'cos I'd done it loads of times. I kind of knew that getting fussy about what you heard [from] the bass end on the bass drum was completely a non-starter 'cos you couldn't hear any bass in there anyway. But this just did not work with the collective thing of an unhappy Jimmy and an unhappy Mick and ...".

Though the Stones and Miller were not blaming Chkiantz for the shortcomings of what they were hearing, the fact that the more experienced Smith was around led them to take the decision to ask him to take over from Chkiantz. Chkiantz was furious, both at the decision and the results that Smith proceeded to come up with. Chkiantz, "I was angry about it for ages. I felt I wasn't given a chance and what he did on that was kind of like forcing the sound through. Which I suppose was a pragmatic approach but if felt very much that all the stuff that we'd been trying to do on the whole of this album had been betrayed by this track. Vic was very much into doing his own productions and Peter Sarstedt and stuff like that and what's he got to do with the Stones, kind of thing. He just did all kind of things that I'd been fighting not to do and they loved it. Heavy limiting and drums and stuff like that. He just put together a thing which at the time sounded to me like, 'Yeah, sure, that's how you record Peter Sarstedt.' I was totally fucking emotively involved and upset and oh dear, oh dear." Time has dimmed Chkiantz's anger and he is now able to see the same qualities of this recording that so many millions of others do. "It's curious—I actually like the track now. Probably 'cos I didn't do anything on it! I don't know why I got so [angry]. I think I was on one of those stupid dead-loss situations for myself which you should never really get into but happens ... But I still think that the Stones would never have been happy in that studio. I don't think they ever used it again voluntarily, if at all."

"Monkey Man" saw Bill Wyman playing the vibraphone. Colloquially referred to as "vibes", it looks like an electronic xylophone but with tubular resonators and a motor-driven rotating vane that give a vibrato effect. After initial work on "Monkey Man" was done on April 17–22, the band came back to it from June 10 to July 2.

April may also have seen the recording of several Jagger/Richards songs to which there are no dates attached, all of them unreleased, at least under the titles they were initially given: "Curtis Meets Smokey", "Mucking About", "So Fine", "Toss The Coin", "The Vulture", and "When Old Glory Comes Along". However, we do know for certain that April 23 saw a remarkable jam session take place at Olympic that featured Ry Cooder, Nicky Hopkins, and all of the Stones except Richards. Some have suggested that Richards stayed away from the session because he had fallen out with Cooder (possibly about who originated the riff of "Honky Tonk Women"). Whatever the reason for his absence, musicians are hardly inclined to sit twiddling their thumbs when waiting on a colleague, and this stellar line-up of talent began whiling away the hours with a jam, or "blow".

Chkiantz was engineering that day. "Sometimes the blows are really good," he says. "Studio engineers love blows because it's normally a great time to get the sound sorted out. Now I prefer people to blow for a couple of hours while I sort the general sounds out and get everything working, and it loosens them up. And they're not 'supposed' to be playing something—because one of the things that really

112

get in the way of making the record that counts is the intention of making the record that counts. It's a difficult trick." He continues of the April 23 session, "We were all there. I can't remember what got it started. It was an evening. First thing is that things were set up to go on working because as we were waiting the sounds were at least more or less nominally put together. I think it just started as a sort of 'Do you remember this?' ... It was great. It was a really good fun jam. It was a great session. It was farting around. It was just they got into a good thing. When it starts off with that da-da-da-da-deh, that was just a joke and you can hear Mick being bossy-boots—'Too bangy'—but that's the one piece I really love on that, the way he turned that around, the way the rhythm turned around is exactly fucking brilliant, and that was Nicky Hopkins."

Belatedly, and somewhat bizarrely considering the completed, unreleased songs they had in the vaults, the band chose to release the results of this blow in January 1972 as the album *Jamming With Edward*. Though Chkiantz is correct in stating that it has many enjoyable qualities to it, Jagger provided a sleevenote to the release that seemed to drip with contempt for the product and the people purchasing it, "It was promptly forgotten (which may have been for the better) until it was unearthed from the family vaults. As it cost about $2.98 to make the record, we thought that a price of $3.98 was appropriate for the finished product. I think that that is about what it is worth. No doubt some stores may even give it away. I hope you spend longer listening to this record than we did making it." (Some might suggest that it is attitudes like that which meant that punk had to happen.) Chkiantz at least was pleased with its appearance. "We'd all been hustling about somebody ought to do something about that. It was great and we all enjoyed listening to it. I think everybody loved it. It was good fun, that was all. Kind of, why not?"

April 23 also saw the band tackle "Lyle Street Lucie", a Bill Wyman song they had first attempted to record during the *Beggars Banquet* sessions. Though a Wyman composition, the song featured a Jagger vocal sung in what we would now called Mockney (mock Cockney). The track has an acoustic flavor. It's diverting enough—and when it explodes into the up-tempo section is exciting—but its stop-start structure and whimsical nature ultimately render it cast-off material. This is what it became. Eventually, it was released (as "Down Town Suzie") on *Metamorphosis*.

Cooder would not work with the Stones again. In 1970, his fury at the band—or more specifically Richards— splattered the pages of *Rolling Stone* magazine, where he said, "The Rolling Stones brought me to England under totally false pretences. They weren't playing well and were just messing around the studio. When there'd be a lull in the so-called rehearsals, I'd start to play my guitar. Keith Richard would leave the room immediately and never return. I thought he didn't like me! But as I found out later, the tapes would keep rolling. I'd ask when we were going to do some tracks. Mick would say, 'It's alright Ry, we're not ready yet.' In the four or five weeks I was there, I must have played everything I know. They got it all down on these tapes. Everything". Cooder also alleged that the riff of "Honky Tonk Women" was based on one of his progressions.

"I heard those things he said—I was amazed," Richards later said. "I learned a lot of things off a lot of people." However, he did acknowledge that his decision to switch from a six-string to a five-string guitar style was picked up from Cooder.

"It sounds to me like it's kind of inevitable," says Chkiantz of Cooder's rip-off allegations, adding, "Generally." He elucidates, "Let's play devil's advocate a moment. Here you are, you're Keith, you've got this guy in 'cos you like what he does and what you saw him do. He plays some stuff but one way and another you don't see him fitting in the band. You've given him a starting grid, as it were. He's played some stuff along. It's kind of okay but not really what you wanted. You toy with the idea of getting him to do it, come to the conclusion that it's hopeless and it's going to be easier to learn how to do it. This little twiddle that he did there or that bit there, that was a really good idea but the rest of it wasn't and the structure and format are different so you do that. Who owns it? Who's right? You could well see that he had a right to [think] the guy's ripped him off, that the other guy just used him. I don't think that he went actively and ripped him off. I don't think he employed him with the sole intention of picking up what he could learn. I just don't read him that way. I can see how after the event, a disgruntled Ry Cooder—or, incidentally, anybody—could feel that this had happened, and I'm quite sure that if I was in their shoes, I would have more than just a suspicion. But I don't think from where I sit that I do see it entirely like that."

In addition to feeling ripped off, Altham remembers Cooder also being unhappy with the remuneration he received for "Love In Vain", the one track on *Let It Bleed* on which they did use one of his contributions. Altham explains "Something Stu said. I was very close to Stu. I used to see him at the weekends in the pub and things and it was some little time after it but apparently he was moaning and groaning that he hadn't been paid a proper royalty or hadn't been paid what he was promised or something and he'd come over especially for it, etc. etc. He didn't come over especially for it actually but that's another story. I think Keith got a bit upset about it."

According to Bill Wyman's book *Rolling With The Stones*, in early May Keith Richards played bass on "That's The Way God Planned It", a recording by Billy Preston laid down at Trident Studios. However, Vic Smith, who engineered on the day, insists that in fact Klaus Voorman was the bassist.

On May 28, Mick and Marianne were busted at their Chelsea home. It followed an incident in the King's Road about a week before when Jagger's car had been stopped by the police and two officers had demanded the right to search it. Jagger refused on the lack of reasonable grounds and called his solicitor. The raid bore some of the dubious hallmarks of the recent prosecution of Brian Jones: the same police officer was in charge of both cases and the circumstances were adamantly disputed. Though the case wouldn't come to court until December, when it did Jagger not only effectively accused the police of lying about the incidents involved in the raid—he was supposed to have shouted from outside the house that Marianne should hide the "weed"; Jagger retorted that he would not use a word like "weed" as it was archaic and that, in any case, "someone" had a hand over his mouth—it was also alleged that the police had offered to drop the case if Jagger bribed them. Jagger was up for this—another bust might put him in the same bracket as Brian Jones: unable to get a visa into America and thus scuppering any chance of the Stones touring there—but the deal supposedly fell through. After the case—thankfully for the band held after the American tour—Jagger was fined for cannabis possession and Faithfull was acquitted.

Meanwhile, at Olympic, the long and tortuous process of perfecting "Honky Tonk Women" was continuing.

It had gone through a lot of changes since the band first tackled the song in the second week of March (Bill Wyman has suggested May 12 as the start date but other known facts call this into question) and even more since Keith had first been inspired to write a Hank Williams-type cowboy ditty in Brazil. It was now a sensual hard-rock track with a picaresque lyric detailing the exploits of a man who is fornicating his way round the world: encountering a gin-soaked bar-room queen in Memphis, meeting a divorcée in New York City, etc. Strangely, the protagonist is not exactly a predatory type, the lyric casting him more as a willing victim, with women throwing him across their shoulders and blowing his nose for him.

This erotic travelog differed at one point from the familiar version, for there is a recording of the track featuring a second verse set in Paris where Jagger speaks, instead of the divorcée in N.Y., of strolling on the boulevards of Paris as naked as the day that he will die, and observing that though the sailors are so charming there in Paris, he just can't seem to "sail you off my mind". The

Stones actually played the song live with this alternate, sexually ambiguous second verse for a while. On this version, incidentally, one can hear far more clearly elements of the recording that would be mixed to near-inaudibility on the finished product. The cowbell is not merely an intro piece but persists. Barrelhouse piano from Stewart can be heard in the choruses and instrumental break. "He had the feel," says Smith of Stewart. "He could lock in to the music and play really cool rhythms and could just hang in and play for hours and hours. He really enjoyed it and I thought it was a cool thing to do actually, to bring Ian in like that. It fitted, so we persevered and got the sound. Sometimes over quite a long period of time, just jamming until the music kind of locked in and once it had locked in it was there. Ian would just really gel with the band. He used to jam with them a lot." Though Stewart was indeed an able pianist, his playing on the alternate version of "Honky Tonk Women" frankly sounds rather leaden, particularly in the second half of the song. A straining brass section—a little like the brass playing in *Exile's* "Rocks Off"—can be heard in the latter half of that alternate version of the song, though still not that high in mix. The brass was comprised of session saxophonists Steve Gregory and Bud Beadle. Smith, "[They were] there for all the versions we recorded."

Because Glyn Johns had had to fly to America again to work, it was Vic Smith who was the engineer overseeing the protracted and tortuous development of this track. Alan O'Duffy remembers, "I was in the other room. I remember it taking ages to record. Trying to get different styles or get the right tempo or just faff around for ages and ages. Getting the riff, getting the groove, took a while on 'Honky Tonk Women' 'cos I think they did transmogrify the thing into a different space. It was very commercial. It was rather more commercial when it finished than when perhaps it started as a country song."

"We had to go through the process of completely re-recording the track five times, Smith adds. "Glyn created the very first backing track, then I joined. I completed that recording, which took several weeks. Then we went on to develop the album. We recorded 'Country Honk' then 'Midnight Rambler' and then we cut another full version of 'Honky Tonk Women', which took several more weeks. Once that was mixed we decided to record the song again but this time completely live. The whole process became quite stimulating. So in essence all the musical ideas which had been rehearsed through the other previous recordings were now being put to the live test in the studio. We were recording on eight-track tape, so we could not actually save any vocals or save any guitars: it was either recorded or replaced by another performance. The third, all-live recording was quite an exciting version. After that we attempted another new recording. Then later on during the *Let it Bleed* album recordings we attempted the fifth version. We actually went back to the original bass and drum track and then we rebuilt that again to form the final single."

For Smith, this perfectionism was a revelation. "I as an engineer had not experienced this process before. Artists stated 'We're making a single' and it would be recorded on that day and be mixed the following day, but they had not the luxury of the budget to completely remake it."

"Honky Tonk Women" boasts arguably the most famous cowbell part in rock history. In fact, it is the first sound heard on the finished recording. The part is actually played by Jimmy Miller—something that would no doubt have confirmed Al Kooper's suspicions, had he been there, that Miller was determined to get himself onto the Stones' recordings in some way. A cowbell is in some respects a bizarre instrument. It is exactly what it sounds like. As O'Duffy explains, "A cowbell is a wedge-shaped metal enclosure. It perhaps is four inches across, two inches deep, made out of tin or some sort of light steel. Sometimes it has a handle on the back end, something you could grab onto, and you can mount a cowbell with a clamp onto a drum kit. The original idea of the cowbells was that they'd clang if you had two of them together as the cows walked along, they just banged together. It was to warn the shepherd or the cow-handler or whatever that the cows were moving: you'd hear it across the valley. That was when you had two cowbells together. So take one cowbell off and hit it with something metal or a bit of wood and you'd get that noise that we had on 'Honky Tonk Women'. But just using one of them with a drumstick would create what Jimmy Miller did. It's a common enough usage in percussion."

O'Duffy doesn't recall the exact moment it was decided to use a cowbell but thinks it an unsurprising idea to emerge in the studio environment that Miller would create. "It was just a case of 'What's the tempo?' or 'What's the feel?' or 'How do we get this?' and 'Why don't we try a cowbell?'" he says. "Jimmy was a fantastic, mad, groovy guy. He was just a great encouraging, mad fellow. I remember seeing Jimmy

Miller play it actually. He plays the cowbell in front of Charlie and the band were lined up in front of us." Vic Smith adds, "It just seemed to be very much part of the arrangement. As soon as we'd start laying yet another track down, Jimmy was just out there. It was a rhythm pattern that Charlie and Jimmy had worked up together and the only difficulty was finding the right place for Jimmy to stand 'cos he didn't have his own mic. It was just literally picking up on the overhead drum mic and all the drums went down mixed to one track and that was it."

As well as the cowbell, the percussion track on "Honky Tonk Women" is remarkable for the cavernous sound of Charlie Watts's drum work, especially in the opening moments when the drums and cowbell are the only instruments heard. Smith explains, "It's very much the sound of the room really and not miked too close but to have a balance between the direct sound and capturing some of the acoustics from the room. [Studio 1] had that fantastic sound which George himself expanded on when he worked with Zeppelin: he had the mic up in the roof for the Bonham drums, so he was using that room to the full extent." O'Duffy says, "I think it's to do with the fact that maybe there were other microphones open in the room and you had that eighty-foot ceiling and you can hear the sound of the kit coming through the cowbell microphone for one thing, so it gives more space to the sound. There's more air around the sound of that kit. Charlie would have been on a rostrum possibly in the middle of the room, twenty foot, thirty foot back from the windows of the control room in the middle of the studio."

In *According To The Rolling Stones*, Watts said, "We've never played an intro to 'Honky Tonk Women' like the way it is on the record. That's Jimmy playing the cowbell and either he comes in wrong or I come in wrong—but Keith comes in right, which makes the whole thing right. It's actually a mistake but from my point of view it works." "Exactly," O'Duffy agrees. "It isn't a one, two, three, four, dah dah da da dah. It was a strange one. But it's this wonderful world of Jimmy Miller. It's this thing of following a groove, that's the story."

For both Smith and Keith Richards, the song underwent its most important transformation when Mick Taylor joined the group. "He definitely was an enormous addition to the band," recalls Smith of Taylor's arrival. "It just felt like he was there to stay." Taylor's first session with the Rolling Stones was on May 31. It was an underhand move by a band who had not yet told Brian Jones that his services would no longer be required.

The Brian Jones problem had become even more visible upon his return from Joujouka. An eager Jones is reported to have asked Jagger in one late April session, "What can I play?," to which Jagger acidly responded, "I don't know. What can you play?" It was a cruel putdown from a man with only an ounce of Jones's remarkable talent, but a perhaps understandable eruption of frustration at difficult, even insufferable, behavior from Jones that had now been rumbling on for several years. Dave Hassinger—who engineered for the Stones in the mid-Sixties—recalls Jones being difficult even during his tenure as producer, and his colleagues reacting to it with almost saintly forbearance. "Brian was there sometimes and not there sometimes," says

Hassinger. "He'd come to a session and just lay down on the floor and stare at the ceiling and everybody'd just take a break until he would leave. That's one thing I really admire about the Stones. There was never any confrontations. I never saw an argument between any of them."

Yet whatever his dilettante attitudes, for a long time dismissing Brian would have been inconceivable, not just to the band themselves (the ties forged by Brian, Mick, and Keith having lived together in solidarity-building dues-paying squalor in Chelsea in the early days were not easily forgotten) but to the public: Brian had always been an articulate spokesman for the group and had an undeniable glamour that none of them could match.

"Brian was definitely getting more and more un-together," says Chkiantz of Jones's behavior at the *Let It Bleed* sessions. "He was definitely getting more and more hopeless. It's funny the way musicians go actually. I remember him having to explain to me in some detail [about] some bloody hand drum that he'd decided he'd wanted to play and he'd been plonked into the isolation booth. Brian on some track on *Let It Bleed* was [hitting] these I think Moroccan or African drums— white-skinned things—and he wanted to use those because he thought that Charlie was out of time. This is from somebody who couldn't walk across a floor. He thought that if he played slightly off the beat, then if the mix was right that would sort of pull Charlie forward. And you're thinking, 'First, he isn't out of time, secondly, if he is then that's easy, we do another take.' I think Brian must have been able to tell. Behind it all I'm sure Brian must have been aware that they were edging him out ... On the other hand I suppose in a strange kind of way I just couldn't conceive of the Stones without Brian so it never occurred to me that they would be looking for somebody else. It's kind of like one of those awful, hopeless sort of things but it never occurred to me. I don't think I really thought about it."

Vic Smith agrees that the notion of the Stones without Brian at that point was inconceivable. Keith Altham, however, completely disagrees with that. "It didn't seem like that at all. It seemed to me actually that he would be pretty much replaced fairly soon. 'Cos he didn't seem to me to have a grip on anything any more and I thought that was going to happen, I really did. He was just fading away, getting paler and paler and less involved in anything that was going on. I don't think anyone ever said [to me], 'We're going to aim Brian out of the band' but I think things were said [like], 'How much longer can he last as an integral member?'" He adds, "I remember Brian saying things [in] interviews, things that were kind of strange like, 'I've had an offer to join The Beatles.' Now whether he had an offer to join The Beatles or whether he hadn't, I don't know. Probably was in his imagination. Probably talked to John Lennon, they're both out of their heads [and John said] 'You should come and join us.' I somehow thought actually Brian should have been a Beatle and John Lennon should have been a Rolling Stone, personally. Just a fancy of mine. Brian really wanted fame and celebrity, wanted to be a star, and Lennon really wanted to be a kind of activist and I think he'd have had far more chance in the Stones than he actually had in The Beatles. But that's another line of inquiry, as they say."

It's conceivable that the Stones would have hung in there for Brian—waited to see whether he could get his creative juices flowing again—were it not for the necessity to get some money flowing into the coffers. The surest way to do this in the rock marketplace is to tour America. As mentioned earlier, Jones would not have been able to take part in any such venture because of his drug convictions. It's impossible to know what was going through Jagger's mind at this point, but one wonders what kind of pang his own recent bust must have caused his conscience. After all, if the allegations he later made were true, that put him in the same boat as Jones: potentially unable to tour the States because of a conviction resulting from a frame-up. If he did, he clearly brushed it aside, and it is perhaps not for anyone who did not experience Jones's exasperating behavior first-hand to draw any adverse moral conclusions from it.

In Sixties rock, there seemed to be two musical schools from which virtuoso guitarists emerged. If The Yardbirds were the university (Eric Clapton, Jeff Beck, and Jimmy Page passing through their ranks, making classic records on the way), then John Mayall's Bluesbreakers were the secondary school, grooming the talents of brilliant young axe-slingers like Eric Clapton, Peter Green, and Mick Taylor before they moved upward into bigger bands. (Consistent with his contrary nature at the time, Clapton actually executed a reverse trajectory, going from the university to the secondary school, quitting The Yardbirds in disgust at their commerciality and fleeing to the more purist Mayall.) In May 1969, Mick Taylor was a 21-year-old guitarist who had been playing in the Bluesbreakers for two years. At the time, he

was actually surplus to the Bluesbreakers' requirements—
Mayall having decided on a new acoustic musical avenue in
which a virtuoso electric guitarist was not needed—so when
Mick Jagger made a call to Mayall asking about guitarists,
Mayall was pleased to be able to recommend the man he was
making redundant.

Vic Smith reports that Taylor didn't seem nervous when
he began playing with the group, "He was a fresh new face in
the camp and he was just kind of in there hard-working, just
laying some down." Perhaps this was due to the fact that
when Taylor turned up at Olympic on that first day, he had
no idea that it was anything more than session work. "I was
invited to do a session with the Stones," Taylor later said. "It
puzzled me, I had never met Mick Jagger in my life and here
he was phoning me. I went down and played on some tracks
and thought little more about it. Then they asked me if I
wanted to be a Stone. I was amazed. Brian Jones was leaving,
I was told. [The first song I worked on with the Stones] was
called 'Live With Me', very appropriately named because
once I joined the Stones, it was like living with a family for
the next five or six years. It was an interesting session,
actually, because they were putting the finishing touches on
Let It Bleed and the first track I played on was 'Live with Me'.
We did that live, and the second thing I did was I overdubbed
my guitar part on 'Honky Tonk Women'."

Many expressed puzzlement that the Rolling Stones—
who could have virtually any guitarist in the world they
wanted—should choose not a well-known sessioner like Al
Kooper or Ry Cooder nor a fellow star like Eric Clapton or
Gram Parsons but an unknown kid. Keith Altham has a

theory. "I think they thought he was very gifted and very controllable. Wasn't going to cause them any problems. And he didn't, did he?" When Taylor joined, he certainly seemed incredibly young and innocent in the context of the Stones' relatively weathered faces and massively weathered reputations. However, Taylor has subsequently denied the story put about at the time—and repeatedly endlessly in biogs since—that he was a teetotal vegetarian when he joined. Either way, there was a mellifluous, blues-tinged maturity to his guitar style that belied his fresh-faced looks. It was the first and last time the Stones would employ a virtuoso player in one of the guitarist's roles. For one person who had worked closely with the band, this very virtuosity was something that made his appointment inappropriate. Chkiantz says, "I don't think I ever thought it was really a good idea. Just didn't think he was the right person. Possibly, he was too good a musician, kind of thing. But, look, I had all kind of crazy ideas."

Richards later said, several years after Taylor's five-and-a-half-year stint in the group was over, "My playing relationship with Mick Taylor was always very good. There is no way I can compare it to playing with Brian, because it had been so long since Brian had been interested in the guitar at all, I had almost gotten used to doing it all myself—which I never really liked. I couldn't bear being the only guitarist in a band, because the real kick for me is getting those rhythms going, and playing off of another guitar. But I learned a lot from Mick Taylor, because he is such a beautiful musician. I mean, when he was with us, it was a time when there was probably more distinction, let's say, between rhythm guitar and lead guitar than at any other time in the Stones. More than now and more than when Brian was with us, because Mick Taylor is that kind of a player; you know he can do that."

Even if we accept Altham's theory about the Stones' rationale for Taylor's employment, it can't be denied that he would turn out to be amazingly influential on the band's sound—possibly far more than he has ever been given credit for. For what we now consider to be the classic, generic Rolling Stones sound—that riff-driven, scruffy but propulsive and slightly decadent rock 'n' roll style—only really came into being when Taylor joined the group. Had the Stones ceased to exist at the same time The Beatles did, we would remember them the way we do the Fab Four: as a group whose only defined style was their sheer eclecticism, with each album (and single) sounding totally different to its predecessor. The Rolling Stones sound as we know it is Mick Taylor's sound, as defined and refined on *Sticky Fingers* and *Exile On Main Street*.

For Smith, Taylor's contribution to "Honky Tonk Women" was the golden touch for that track. "He joined only on the last version," says Smith. "When Mick and Keith developed that guitar line leading into the chorus the music just lifted, and I think that's where the whole track kicked into sounding like an amazing single; it just added so much magic. I very much remember when they were rehearsing those lead lines that come before the chorus—twining together, duet guitars, it was gorgeous." Taylor later said, "I definitely added something to 'Honky Tonk Women,' but it was more or less complete by the time I arrived and did my overdubs. They had already laid down the backing track, but it was very rough and incomplete. I added some guitars to it, but I didn't play the riffs that start it—that's Keith playing. I played the country kind of influence on the rock licks between the verses."

The Stones' erratic and unpredictable schedules meant that Vic Smith very often had downtime in the studio during the genesis of the track. He says, "They'd say they were coming in at seven o'clock, then arrive at midnight. They'd work from midnight to four but the engineer and Jimmy, we always had to be there when they turned up." Enterprisingly, Smith—who was also a songwriter on the side—filled the time by composing on a piano with his friend Canadian singer Nanette Workman. On one evening, the two decided to lay off the songwriting and go out to the movies, secure in the knowledge that there was next to no chance that the band would arrive before the picture was over. Naturally, Sod's Law kicked into operation. Smith recalls, "We got back at eleven o'clock and they'd been there since ten, so all the Stones were there and Jimmy and everyone was pushing all the knobs on the desk with the 'Honky Tonk Women' track. It was quite amusing. The speakers were distorting and all the faders were at the max. Everybody was having a go. I felt seriously embarrassed. I just had to take over and pull everything back to zero and rebuild the mix." The Stones, he reports, accepted the incident with reasonable good humor.

In fact, the occasional presence of Workman in the studio actually proved providential for everyone concerned. As Smith recalls, "She was a fantastic vocalist and when one of the band heard her, she ended up singing the backing vocal with Mick on 'Honky Tonk Women.' She really had a stunning voice. The harmony vocal was I believe intended for Keith, but Nanette just gave it that cutting edge."

"Keith played bass on 'Honky Tonk Women'," reveals O'Duffy. "Fabulous bass player. We did that in studio 3. Studio 3 was really an add-on. It was the smallest of the three. It was really good for vocal overdubs. Studio 3 was unique at Olympic because you could see the sky, you could see the outside. The other studios were boxes where you couldn't see the world. It's quite funny, 'cos the bass doesn't come in till halfway through the record on the chorus."

O'Duffy says he doesn't know quite why Bill Wyman did not play bass on the finished record. Marianne Faithfull went so far as to aver in her autobiography, "Keith always did the bass lines. I think the only reason they had Bill Wyman in the band was because they needed someone to play bass on tour." Considering that Wyman was one half of one of rock history's most acclaimed rhythm sections and is responsible for some of rock's greatest bass parts—especially the rapid-fire work at the end of "19th Nervous Breakdown"—this seems improbable, even though Richards is known to have played bass on some Stones tracks. For his part, Smith says, "Didn't happen while I was there. [Bill] was solid actually and had a very individual sound." Chkiantz agrees with Smith, "I think it may have happened once or twice. It was a lot easier to overdub bass than it was to overdub drums. I certainly don't recall it being a regular occurrence. Keith sometimes thought he had to do everything. You have to remember also that there was every possibility that even if Keith did overdub bass or something, that Bill would overdub it back. Don't think these things didn't get redone and redone and redone." He does add, "On *Beggars Banquet* it is true that Keith played bass on some of the basic acoustic put-together tracks and Bill did percussion."

With all the components in place, including a typically bellowed, insouciant vocal from Jagger, attention now focused on mixing, a task handled again by Smith. "I mixed it after a long, long process," he says. "I was never quite sure when we had finished the single as we recorded it so many times. In the mixing room at the back of Olympic Studios it was about eleven or midnight and we'd been mixing 'Honky Tonk' all that day. Mick and Keith and Jimmy said, 'Look, we need a break so we're going to go for a walk around Barnes Common' and they headed off together for a walkabout." In their absence, Smith decided to do something experimental. "I was looking for an original sound to add to Mick's voice. I tried a wacky effect which I was told off for by the maintenance people at the studio later on. I used a tape delay to help Mick's voice sit into the track and I further enhanced the sound by winding editing tape around the capstan motor, producing a warbling effect on the voice as the tape passed through but ruining reels of tape in the process but it produced the desired effect. That was the sound incorporated in the final mix. A primitive delay effect." When they came back from their twilight-hours stroll around Barnes Common, the Jagger, Richards, and Miller triumvirate liked what they heard. "Mixes can just suddenly develop in the studio after hours or sometimes even weeks of working," says Smith. "The final mix had the impact, color, and energy to have the success that it did … I took the final mono master tape to the Decca cutting room the next day and cut the vinyl master for release ... Mick, Keith, and Jimmy were a highly critical team and they were searching for the ultimate recording and mix and I felt the mix they chose truly represented the song and the arrangement they had put together. It definitely had all the magic. When Mick Taylor joined them and when Nanette added her vocal with Mick [Jagger] it just added that little bit of extra spice to the final single."

Smith's latter comments are slightly curious, for the strange thing about "Honky Tonk Women" is that the female vocals—and the brass section—are almost inaudible, mixed so far down that they are merely indistinct dabs of coloration. Though the artistic power and commercial success of "Honky Tonk Women" can't be denied, it does seem strange that the Stones should invest time, money, and effort in dubbing on vocals and horns that add little or nothing to the final result. This propensity to pick the "wrong" mix is something that has caused no little anguish down the years to George Chkiantz. While not necessarily expressing dissatisfaction with the mix of "Honky Tonk Women", Chkiantz says of Jagger, "He'll go along and we'll all spend for ever and ever and ever mixing and remixing tracks and thinking we've done really well or not done really well or what have you, then he'll take it off to be cut and then suddenly right at the last minute he'll panic, decide he's got to change everything and book sessions in whatever studio he can find. As it's last-minute, it's anywhere, and then he'll go off with whatever particular thing he's got in mind and all the rest of us who've [been] sweating our guts out on the album will be in fucking tears. 'Where has it all gone?' Just couldn't understand why. Normally what Mick did when in doubt [is] turn Keith up. Which is why it would take me several years before I could comfortably listen to a Stones album because I had to forget about all the stuff I knew was on it and was missing. Because there's some brilliant stuff that just got left out or marginalized and there was probably room on the tracks for it." However, he does concede an important point. "Other people have all got theories about how the Stones should make their music but strangely enough they don't bring out the big bucks, do they? There's thousands of people around the musical business who see the Stones going in [and say], 'Ooh I can't understand why they take so many takes,' 'Surely it's not necessary to do this,' 'Surely you could do that,' 'So inefficient.' But actually the most inefficient way of making records is making records that didn't sell. Nothing was more expensive than that."

Asked if all this hard work on "Honky Tonk Women" was done because it was always earmarked for single release, Smith says, "Songs develop into singles in the studio. It always sounded like a single from the first recording [but] the hard work just meant we were searching for the best performance and the best results."

"Live With Me", Taylor's Stones baptism, was less special than "Honky Tonk Women". Another up-yours to the outmoded morality that was still prevalent in certain quarters, which frowned on Faithfull's pregnancy. Jagger's lyric milks this to the utmost. Trying to persuade the object of his affections to join his household, he admits to "nasty habits" and portrays an abode of unruly children and sexually degenerate staff. The line "My best friend he shoots water rats and feeds 'em to his geese" was inspired, according to Tony Sanchez, by a grotesque sight Jagger had been confronted with when visiting Richards's home: Richards and Sanchez had shot four rats that lived on the moat around his country house and hung them on a fence. For some reason, Hopkins' piano was beefed up by the piano of Leon Russell, at least according to the album's sleeve credits, whichalso state that Russell arranged the horns on the track.

"Country Honk" was first recorded on May 12. This version lacked the fiddle part heard on the new version that would be recorded when the Stones decamped to the States at the year's end. Smith says "I think it came during [the genesis of 'Honky Tonk Women'], when we were about three or four versions into the track. I think we recorded it before we finished the final mix on the single. It was a variation of the song, the theme. It became very much a part of the album. I thought it was great at the time. Loved it."

a new era

With Taylor having been formally asked to join the band, there remained for the Rolling Stones the not inconsiderable matter of informing founder member and one-time friend Brian Jones that he was out of the band.

To their credit, it was something not done over the phone or by letter. Instead, Jagger, Richards, and Watts journeyed together to Jones's country house to deal with this grisly necessity. It's a measure of just how profound was the act they were performing that they had decided to cushion the blow with a quite remarkably generous severance package. Jones would receive an initial payment of £100,000—a massive sum for those days—plus £20,000 a year as long as the Stones lasted.

Jones apparently took the decision stoically. "The fact that he was expecting it made it easier," Richards later said. "He wasn't surprised."

Wyman later claimed that Jones knew by now of the fact that Taylor had been auditioned. Altham suggests, "I think in some ways he did want to be out because it was a relationship that was so painful to him which he wasn't a part of and couldn't be a part of, that maybe he was better off trying to do something on his own or with somebody else."

The whole wretched task had passed off in a more gentlemanly fashion than probably anyone was expecting, and this civility underscored the comments by the respective parties when the announcement was made on

June 8 1969 that Brian was no longer a Rolling Stone. The respective statements may well have been the very first "artistic differences" explanation given for a rock musician departing his band. Like all such explanations, it was complete baloney. The Stones said, "Brian wants to play music which is more his own rather than always playing ours ... but we part on the best of terms." Jones offered, "I no longer see eye to eye with the others over the discs we are cutting. We have agreed that an amicable termination of our relationship is the only answer."

Apart from the drug charge and possible visa-denying conviction hanging over Jagger's head, the final hurdle to a new Rolling Stones—a Rolling Stones Mach II as Richards had put it lately—was now out of the way. The Stones certainly felt they were on a creative roll. June was the month that an announcement was made that the band would be releasing two albums this year: one (to be entitled *Sticky Fingers*) in September and another in December. This almost actually came to pass—an 8-track acetate of the former was prepared—and it's possible that only a disinclination to let Allen Klein's publishing company have so many of their songs when they were trying to disentangle themselves from him that prevented it happening.

Jones himself—after so long artistically comatose—seemed reinvigorated. He contacted Alexis Korner—one of the kingpins of the UK blues scene that the Stones had once been the darlings of—to help him direct his musical visions which, according to Korner, revolved around the kind of back-to-basics rock of the likes of the Allman Brothers and Creedence Clearwater Revival. Despite his difficult nature, Jones was a well-loved figure in the music community. To quote Chkiantz, "When he was not out of his head, he was delightful and considerate and all kinds of things you really wouldn't have dreamt of." Jimi Hendrix, John Lennon, and Pete Townshend were all friends and it was perfectly conceivable that Jones would have assembled an all-star cast for his next band and even that it would have made great music.

Mick Taylor was introduced to the public as the new Rolling Stone at a press conference on June 13 in London's Hyde Park. The venue had been chosen because by now the Stones had arranged to play their first gig with the new line-up at that venue. Jagger had been impressed by the recent free gig at Hyde Park given by new supergroup Blind Faith. (Incidentally, it may be the case that the only reason that Eric Clapton was not given the job in the Stones that was ultimately offered to Taylor was because he had just committed himself to Blind Faith. However, Clapton's and Richards's recollections seem to differ.)

The Stones' gig—also free—was scheduled for July 5, the day after the release of "Honky Tonk Women" as their new single, their first U.K. 45 since "Jumpin' Jack Flash" more than a year previously. On the flip of "Honky Tonk Women" was "You Can't Always Get What you Want", albeit, for space reasons, minus the choral introduction that would grace the album version. The track also now featured a melancholy French horn part played by Al Kooper. Kooper says of Jagger, "He called me about nine months [after the original session] in America and said,'I remember that you said you would put horns on that track.' I said, 'Oh yeah.' He said,

'Well we would like you to do that. We're going to send you the tapes and just go ahead and do it.' I was quite surprised that he remembered that I said that."

Chkiantz recalls, "The 24-track [sic] was sent over, because we had to make a separate safety copy and that was a drama all on its own. Actually getting a copy that was a copy. I think the master went over and not the copy and those parts were dubbed on it and then it came back. I remember definitely feeling that flying 'You Can't Always Get What You Want' over to the States and back to put what seemed like a relatively simple horn part on, I really thought it was extraordinary that we couldn't have done that over here. Now I love the part. I could see that it was a good part but it did seem a bit extraordinary and a very risky procedure." Although the safety copy provided some kind of security in the event of the master tape going missing or getting damaged, it would have been one generation of aural quality down from the original.

"I knew exactly what I wanted to do," says Kooper. "It was the same thing that was in my mind when I told them that nine months earlier. The track hadn't changed that much. In fact I had a bad night in the studio. I could not get the horns to play like the Memphis Horns, which is what I wanted, and so it wasn't very good. I put a horn section on: I think three saxes and two trumpets and a French horn. I just played French horn. That was what I originally played on the organ and so I took the organ out and just replaced it with the French horn because there was a much better color after the singing was on it." Kooper sent the tape back to the Stones in London, from whom he reports he "didn't hear a peep."

When the track did appear, he found that the Stones had elected not to use any of his brass section except for the French horn. "Actually I was quite glad," he says. "I thought that Jagger showed impeccable taste by doing that because as I said I had a very bad night in the studio."

"It's a lush track," says Chkiantz of the finished product. "I just like it as a song. I like it because there's a tinge of tragedy in it. There's a sadness in it which I find appealing as a texture. It can't all just be cheerful and so on otherwise you'd just wind up with teenybop stuff. It's got a grace. It's got a rhythm but it's placed at you very beautifully. If you go back through the Stones albums, they've always done a bit of an extravaganza of one kind or another ... I never thought they wrote to order. I never thought at the time that there was a menu but in fact there must have been a background scheme of things because if you look back through the albums actually, the albums very much do take a pattern. In broad strokes, over quite a long period of time, there is a sort of pattern to a Stones album. There's always going to be one long saga track, there's going to be a couple of Dylany type things." Kooper says, "I was so happy about 'You Can't Always Get What You Want' and of course it's become a classic. It's nice to have played on that and I actually often do it in my live show."

The Stones also did some work at Olympic on June 13, although this was probably only mixing and/or overdub work. On June 16, they mimed (though Jagger's vocals were live) to "Honky Tonk Women" and "You Can't Always Get What You Want", for David Frost's television show. Frost also interviewed Jagger.

Though Mick Taylor only appeared on two tracks on *Let It Bleed*, he did actually record several other tracks with the band for the album which didn't make the final cut. For instance, on June 30 the Stones spent an exhausting session at Olympic trying to nail a definitive take of "I Don't Know Why". Written by Stevie Wonder, Paul Riser, Don Hunter, and Lula Hardaway, it was originally released by Wonder on his 1968 album *For Once In My Life*. An anguished song about the pain endured by a protagonist with a feckless and unfaithful lover, it was pretty rich for Jagger to sing such material when—it is reported—at around this juncture he was starting to see actress Marsha Hunt behind Faithfull's back (even though Faithfull admits she had flings with both men and women at the same time). Or would it be making too great a leap in logic to suggest that the anguish he invests in his vocal performance is due (even if subliminally) to the fact that Faithfull was cuckolding him for heroin and other drugs? The Stones clearly felt this song was a genuine contender for the finished record. Taylor contributes some crying guitar lines, Stewart provides piano, and a brass section was even dubbed on at some point, resulting in the version of it that finally ended up on *Metamorphosis* sounding not at all like a standard outtake but like a polished master (which it probably was). It would have made a powerful inclusion on the album. Such a sophisticated and adult view of relationships would have done much to leaven the tiresomely and now datedly provocative nature of some of *Let It Bleed*'s songs.

There are a couple of other, undated, out-takes from the sessions with Taylor involvement. One is "Jiving Sister Fanny", a chugging boogie with a straining vocal that sounds like it's about a groupie. "Fanny" is certainly a female name in Britain—albeit an antiquated one—but composers Jagger and Richards were no doubt not unaware of the word being slang for female genitalia, nor the fact that it was slang for backside in the States. Again, it was clearly not considered a throwaway, with both Hopkins and a brass section featuring. It has a certain pleasant gritty groove but ultimately has that slightly unresolved quality of a song that was never thrashed through by the band enough times for them to find its true shape and iron out its wrinkles. A version ended up on *Metamorphosis*. "I'm Going Down" is a song featuring Rocky Dijon on percussion and (presumably) Bobby Keyes providing fine sax work. It also, for some reason, features Bill Plummer on bass. It has a riff almost like an unstreamlined version of the "Brown Sugar" riff, but Jagger's vocal is too guide-quality to gauge how good the melody line is. Again, it was destined for *Metamorphosis*.

The label—though not the sleeve—of that album attributed "I'm Going Down" to "Jagger/Richard/Taylor," one of only two songs for which Taylor would receive a songwriting credit in his time in the Stones. It was his bitterness over this, according to—amongst others—Tony Sanchez and journalist Nick Kent that led to him quitting the Stones in December 1974. His successor Ronnie Wood has also received mysteriously rare publishing credits since he joined the Stones, despite having been a prolific songwriter on Faces and Rod Stewart albums previously. When I asked Bill Wyman about rumors that Wood got his songs onto Stones albums as long as they were credited to Jagger/Richards and whether he himself would have been prepared to do that, he replied, "Well that's the other alternative. I don't want to go into that. It's a bit political and it's not my business. I'm not like that. I'd rather say, 'No, I'll do it somewhere else.'" Not a definite confirmation but hardly a denial either.

In this regard, the Stones have not lived up to their ideals, which may never have been socialist but were once certainly anti-injustice. It is heartbreaking to read Ronnie Wood justifying Jagger and Richards cheating him out of yet more royalties (for "Black Limousine") in *According To The Rolling Stones*, "One of the lessons I had to learn was that if you want to get a credit, it has to happen there and then in the studio, as you're recording it. I didn't go about it professionally enough to get a credit, so I let it go." However, this is not nearly as heartbreaking as the section where Wood recalls the fact that Mick Taylor had sent them a note in 2003 saying, "I've got no confidence, I'm really depressed and short of cash." "That's all part of what goes with leaving the band," Richards is reported to have remarked on the plight of Taylor who, it should be noted, played on some of the most celebrated and biggest-selling albums of all time and should not have been short of cash in any way, shape or form.

It may also be the case that an undated early version of "Let It Loose"—a song not released until *Exile On Main Street*—was also laid down at around this time.

On July 3, the Stones attended the B.B.C.'s television studios to record a promotional film to be inserted into the channel's chart program Top Of The Pops. Again, this would probably have involved miming. Two clips ended up being shot, and each was shown three times on the program, split across July and August.

There had been some debate about making "You Can't Always Get What You Want" the A-side of the single but in the end the lashing power of "Honky Tonk Women" prevailed. Asked whether he knew "You Can't Always Get What You Want" was considered for the A-side, Smith says, "I didn't, although everybody loved that track. It's quite a dramatic piece. I think looking back that they should have probably been two separate A-sides, but it was a fantastic B-side." Al Kooper, meanwhile, thinks the right track was chosen for the A-side. He was also delighted at the credit he got for the flip. "I was very flattered that they put my name on the label of the single. It said, 'Piano, organ, French horn: Al Kooper.' I was very flattered because most people didn't do that. That was really nice. I really appreciated it. I got to say overall they were very nice to me and treated me quite well any time that I was involved with them. Don't have a bad word to say."

"God, that guy's timing was always dodgy."

Thus spoke Keith Richards in 2003. Just as the dawn of the new Rolling Stones was arriving—two days before the Hyde Park gig, one day before the release of the new single—the news came through that Brian Jones was dead.

On the evening of July 2 1969, Jagger and Richards were in Olympic, putting some overdubs on tracks. As often happened, the work spilled over into the morning of the next day. "I was working with the Stones for this particular week," says Alan O'Duffy. "It was like three in the morning and there was a button on the desk which says 'DIM', which means that it reduces the level of the monitors by 20db, considerable attenuation of the monitors. Hit the button and the whole thing goes quiet. You can still hear what's going on but it just goes quiet. Jimmy and Keith and Mick were in the studio talking away for quite a long time and so rather than sit there and listen to everything and what was going on, you'd give them the respect of hitting the DIM button and think, 'Well when they're ready, they'll give me a shout for what they want to do next.' And then you just thought, 'Well hang on, there's something unusual about this.' So we picked up that there had been a problem with Brian and the phone in the lobby—which was just down to the left of the control room—was ringing and people were on the phone and I know Keith Altham was there and they were on the phone to Keith and at that point I heard that Brian had died, God bless him. This maybe was over the course of an hour. Different phone calls and conversations and everything else."

Keith Altham was there in his role as a journalist. The only night he attended any of the *Let It Bleed* sessions would prove to be unforgettable. "There was all bits and pieces going down and most of the stuff I was listening to when I was there were playbacks," he recalls. "I have a feeling there was a song that was never on the album. I have a feeling it was 'Toss The Coin' or something like that. Jimmy Miller was playing drums at one point in the studio on it. I think Charlie was there." Who told them Brian was dead? "Tom Keylock did," responds Altham, referring to a Stones aide. "He came into the studio. I was sitting in the control room and they were all one by one whisked out of the studio and went into a huddle in the studio outside and it was obviously something very emotive and I wasn't included in on the conversations. They didn't want me there as a journalist I suppose, quite understandably. And then they came back one at a time and gradually I got it out of somebody. I don't know who it was but I got it out of somebody there. It might have been Mick who told me what had happened. Brian had been found dead in the swimming pool. I just went 'Jesus!' You know: What happens now?" And Jagger's response? Altham says, "It was a strange reaction actually. He sort of got angry about it. It was almost like Brian had done it on purpose. Obviously he was upset—they all were, they were all quite shattered by it—and he said something like, 'It goes on, it goes on!'" Considering that they had so recently ejected Jones from the band he formed, the thought must surely at least have crossed their minds—and consciences—that maybe Jones had committed suicide? Altham agrees, "I think it did. Because I don't think anybody at the time was saying how it happened."

O'Duffy adds, "And then what was the most extraordinary thing is that we carried on recording. However they took the news—which was appalling—we carried on doing the vocals, which we had stopped doing. I don't have a comment on that. I just think it's an extraordinary event."

Altham continues, "They carried on doing bits and pieces in the studio for about an hour but then nobody could handle it and everybody drifted out of the studio about two, three in the morning. Keith came up to me and said, 'Look, you won't do anything about this will you until we've been in touch with all the family.' So I said, 'No, of course not.'"

Brian Jones didn't commit suicide. The coroner's verdict was death by misadventure. This may also have been wide of the mark. In subsequent years, a consensus has begun to grow around the idea that Brian was either murdered or died accidentally through malicious horseplay and that the culprit was Frank Thorogood, a builder Jones had recently sacked for his bad attitude but who was still living on the premises and who had been invited to the party Jones had thrown that night. Thorogood confessed to Tom Keylock on his deathbed that he had "done Brian", although some sources say he later retracted this. Jones had apparently invited Thorogood to the party because he could not bear to be on bad terms with anybody. If the Thorogood story is true, how ironic that after all the hurt and distress he had caused others, a streak of essential good nature in Jones should prove his undoing. Whatever Jones's shortcomings, incidentally, it's doubtful that he ever did anything as despicable as the Reverend Hugh Hopkins, who at Jones's memorial hijacked the event to lecture Jones's generation on the alleged error of their ways. When he sternly chided, "Brian was the rebel. He had little patience with authority, convention, tradition. Typical of so many of his generation who have come to see in the Rolling Stones an expression of a whole attitude towards life," it only reinforced the need for the generation of which the Stones were figureheads to kick over the traces.

Despite Mick's "It goes on" reaction, there was discussion of canceling the Hyde Park gig. It was Charlie who suggested that they could still play it as a tribute to Brian. Accordingly, on the afternoon of July 5 1969, the Stones walked out onto the stage at Hyde Park to a crowd of approximately 250,000 people (some estimate half a million), the largest to which they'd ever played up to that point. It might be petty to question, in the circumstances, Jagger's decision to wear a Greek outfit that he knew would look like a dress to many people. After all, this was a rock 'n' roll show and sobriety was never going to be the order of the day. The band made an effort to respect Brian's memory, releasing butterflies in a poetic gesture and Jagger preceding the music by reading a eulogy from Shelley's *Adonais*. They also kicked their set off with "I'm Yours And I'm Hers", an obscure Johnny Winter number that would have caused nothing but blank looks in the crowd but which had been chosen because it had been Jones's current favorite song.

The gig was quite a live baptism for Taylor and quite a comeback show for a band that had not played in public—the *NME* poll-winners' concert and the Rock And Roll Circus excepted—for more than two years. Not surprisingly, they weren't too hot. As well as "I'm Yours And I'm Hers", the Stones performed "Jumpin' Jack Flash", "Honky Tonk Women", "I'm Free", "'Satisfaction" (the latter two their hedonistic, libertarian anthems), "Mercy Mercy", "Down Home Girl", and four tracks from *Beggars Banquet* ("Stray Cat Blues", "No Expectations", "Street Fighting Man", and "Sympathy For The Devil"). They also premiered three still unreleased tracks. It's interesting that "Loving Cup" was one of them. It was certainly attempted during the *Let It Bleed* sessions but would not see the light of day until *Exile On Main Street*. Meanwhile, the two other new tracks, both of which did end up on *Let It Bleed*, were "Love In Vain" and "Midnight Rambler". The latter has yet to be released but the former was included in *Stones In The Park*, a T.V. documentary about the event, and was an electric arrangement that, though raggedy, is actually preferable to the album cut, principally because of Jagger's far more sensitive singing.

The gig was big news. The *London Evening Standard* put out a commemorative edition to celebrate it. Its front-page headline "Stones in the Park" provided the headline for the one-hour documentary on the event by Granada T.V. First broadcast on the commercial channel I.T.V. in September that year, it is now available on D.V.D. Despite the poor sound quality of the Stones on the day, the documentary is an intriguing snapshot of the time, not least in the way one hippie Stones fan explains why the Stones mean more to him than The Beatles, "The Beatles got the M.B.E. but the Stones'd never get anything near it because they're totally anti-establishment."

Brian's funeral was on July 10. Watts and Wyman attended. Jagger and Faithfull, meanwhile, were involved in turmoil on the other side of the world that almost resulted in another death.

The couple had journeyed to Australia to begin shooting the movie *Ned Kelly*. Jagger had the title role as the outlaw who was Australia's equivalent of Jesse James, while Faithfull was scheduled to play his girlfriend. Despite its contempt for the stuffiness of the English, it should be noted that at this point in time, Australia was an extremely conservative country, as English pop groups who had visited it recently had found out. The Small Faces, The Who, and Eric Burdon & The Animals had encountered incredible pettiness from officials and even violence on their recent visits. Coupled with that disdain for English longhairs was wounded national pride on the part of some that a "Pom" had been cast in the role of a man who was to many Australians a folk hero. There were reports in the press at the time that a gang had threatened to kidnap Jagger and cut his long tresses off. (They were actually shorter than usual, cut for the role.) More serious, and ludicrous, was the reaction of Australian police officers when, upon their arrival, Faithfull took a massive overdose of sleeping pills in a suicide attempt. In *Faithfull*, she wrote, "The Sydney police had such a diabolical picture of him they actually believed that Mick had stuffed pills down my throat. And they said, 'Well if it was that, uh, Mick Jag—you can tell us Miss.'"

Marianne Faithfull's life had spun into freefall since her demure beauty had been spotted by Andrew Loog Oldham in 1964 and he had secured her both a recording deal and a new Jagger/Richards song called "As Tears Go By," which became her first hit. The hits had dried up and her reputation—and virginal image—had taken a bruising via her unmarried pregnancy and her appearance in the 1968 soft-porn biker pic *Girl On A Motorcycle*. That her relationship with Jagger was not going well is indicated by her immersion in heroin. Keith Altham observes, "I think Marianne at that time was a very emotional creature and I think lots of things actually affected her that people didn't quite realize did affect her. She was always quite vulnerable, I thought. Brian's death was a kind of final straw. Probably the relationship was difficult, the loss of the child. One of those things alone would be enough to crack somebody up."

Faithfull herself said of her overdose in her autobiography, "I'm ashamed to say that one of the attractions of that way out was ... it would make Mick look particularly bad." Faithfull can't have been unaware that Jagger's previous girlfriend, Chrissie Shrimpton, had tried to commit suicide while in a relationship with him in a virtually identical way. Jagger is condemned now to be remembered as the man whose two successive girlfriends took overdoses, a not altogether fair epitaph considering that, whatever his shortcomings and Faithfull's own heroin use (something she had acknowledged caused him considerable distress), he was hardly a wife-beater or ogre. As Faithfull herself said, "On almost every count Mick behaved like a paragon. He was good to Nicholas and he treated my mother wonderfully. He gave her a thatched cottage … to live in. You couldn't fault him. Maybe that's what irritated me." Write it off as the foolishness of youth. Jagger seems to have: the two are now good friends.

Jagger awoke in the pair's hotel room on the morning of July 8th 1969 to find Faithfull was unconscious. She was in a coma for six days. Her role in *Ned Kelly* was immediately recast, with an Australian actress taking over. Jagger alternated between sitting by her bedside and shooting the movie. His acting in the film was later panned but his state of mind at the time must have been utterly desolate, something not helped by the news flashing around the world and appearing in the headlines. Altham sympathizes "I think losing the baby upset Jagger in quite a considerable way and I think Marianne's attempted suicide really rocked him too."

Despite his traumas—which were added to when he injured his hand shooting one of the film's scenes—Jagger was still one of the all-time great rock artists at the top of his craft, something proved when he used some of his time in Australia to write a new song, ultimately entitled "Brown Sugar", which would be a classic single—although not until

1971—and a perennial Stones anthem. "I wrote 'Brown Sugar' in Australia in the middle of a field," Jagger later recalled. "They were really odd circumstances. I was doing this movie, *Ned Kelly*, and my hand had got really damaged in this action sequence. So stupid. I was trying to rehabilitate my hand and I had this new kind of electric guitar, and I was playing in the middle of the outback and wrote this tune." The track would draw some sort of link between slavery and sex and allude to oral sex. Jagger says, "God knows what I'm on about in that song. It's such a mishmash. All the nasty subjects in one go … I never would write that song now. I would probably censor myself. I'd think, 'Oh God, I can't. I've got to stop.' I can't just write raw like that."

On August 10, Anita Pallenberg gave birth to her and Richards's son, Marlon. Little of the media fuss over Jagger's and Faithfull's unborn child attended this baby born out of wedlock. That Marlon was conceived possibly during—and in any event not long after—Mick's affair with Anita did not affect Richards's delight in being a father. Friends and associates have all testified to his deep love for his son.

In either September or October, Mick Jagger attended Twickenham Studios in Middlesex to record some tracks for the soundtrack of *Ned Kelly*, supervised by Ron Haffkine. The only tracks on which he sang were versions of the traditional song "The Wild Colonial Boy", one of which appeared in the movie, another of which fetched up on the movie soundtrack album.

The first half of October saw the Stones returning the favor (albeit presumably paid) Leon Russell had done them on "Live With Me" by contributing in various ways to tracks he was recording in Olympic. Denny Cordell and Russell were co-producing and Glyn Johns engineering his eponymous album. Watts and Wyman contributed instrumental parts, separately, to a couple of tracks and possibly also played as a duo on another. That other one, which would be an out-take and was not released until 1994, was the Jagger/Richards song "Shine A Light".

the boys in
the back room

So much for the announcement in June that the Stones would be releasing two albums in 1969. Not only had that September release of the album that was to be called *Sticky Fingers* not occurred, but with the first date of the U.S. tour occurring on November 7, there was no way that the new album would be in the stores in time for it. In fact, if the band was to have an album out in 1969 at all, there was now no option but to uproot—including Jimmy Miller and Glyn Johns—and finish it on the other side of the Atlantic.

According to Stanley Booth's book *Dance With The Devil*, (aka *True Adventures Of The Rolling Stones*), the band did some recording in Los Angeles' Sunset Sound Studios. Though he doesn't mention which tracks—apart from witnessing Keith grooving to a playback of "Midnight Rambler"—he is quite specific about this, even stating that because they had no work permits they were having to lock the doors. Bill Wyman also suggests this in his *Rolling With The Stones*. However, Bruce Botnick, then an engineer at Elektra studios, also in L.A., insists that all the American work on *Let It Bleed* was done at his studio. "I don't believe that they recorded at Sunset Sounds," he says. "I'm willing to bet on it. If you look at the credits on the back of the album and it says 'The boys in the back room,' none of those people on there are at Sunset Sounds. I know, 'cos they had just gotten into town and I think they had rented a home and I remember that they were listening to Creedence Clearwater and that's all they were listening to. They were preparing for that tour and they came to Los Angeles and came to Elektra studios because of David Anderley. He was head of A.&R. for Elektra at that time and he was friendly with Mick and with Jimmy Miller, mainly Jimmy Miller. Actually, his really, really good friend was Glyn Johns. It probably came through Glyn that this happened. They came in with the tapes and worked there for about a week."

Botnick is wrong on one detail. Jerry Hansen was another name mentioned on the sleeve and he was an engineer at Sunset Sounds, so there seems to have been at least some work done at the latter studio.

Of Elektra and the kind of facilities it had at the time, Botnick says, "It was the latest and the greatest of that time, the most advanced. It had an English desk in it, which I can't remember the name of right now. And it was heavily modified by our technicians, so it almost wasn't the original desk. There was an entire wall of a Moog synthesizer. And we had custom loudspeakers. We had eight-track. We didn't have sixteen-track, and this album was only recorded in eight-track. I remember they came in with the eight-tracks and the two-track masters." There was only one recording room at Elektra, whose dimensions were approximately 22 by 45 feet, with a 10-foot ceiling.

The work done at Elektra would be minimal but crucial—for instance, a certain vocal *coupe de grace* being applied to "Gimme Shelter". Botnick says "It was obvious they had to get it done, because they were on tour and they had to have an album to tour behind. So they were running a little late, but when they arrived this album was pretty much in place. Everything except for 'Country Honk' was in place—and basically sequenced. What is on the album is what I worked with. We only worked on the songs that were coming out. They did the remixes. I remember removing the old mixes to another reel and inserting the new ones. Mick Taylor did some overdubs. They were pretty efficient. They knew what they had to do. It was mainly all on Mick's [Jagger] shoulders. He had a bunch of vocals he hadn't done and so he got himself up for it and did them and he was very economical and efficient."

Botnick found himself impressed by the Stones' frontman's intelligence. "He's a very smart man," he says of Jagger, whom he had met before. "I've known him for quite a few years and I think he's just a very bright and very creative person. It was very businesslike in the studio. I know this sounds bizarre to imagine because you hear stories about drinking and carrying on, but it wasn't the case this time around." Of Richards, Botnick says, "Found him a very nice man. Actually a historian in relation to music and to where different forms of music, where their derivation came from. We had a conversation about a particular brand of rock 'n' roll and he says, 'Well you know the roots of that come from Scottish type of stuff,' and then he demonstrated it for me."

Of the rhythm section, Botnick recalls of Bill, "Very nice. He didn't have much to do. He was just hanging. Charlie is always great. He didn't have anything to do either, except on 'Country Honk'." Mick Taylor, he says, "was a very nice man. Fell in love with a flying V guitar that we had there but we wouldn't let him keep it. We didn't let anybody walk from the studio with it."

Of the band's production team, Botnick says, "Glyn was the man and he was making it happen and he worked very fast and very efficiently and it was a good creative atmosphere." And Jimmy Miller? Botnick adds. "I thought he was really kind of mellow. It's a balancing act, keeping everybody happy and focused on what had to be done." Though the tour was looming, Botnick discerned no panic in the ranks. "We didn't spend tremendous long hours. It was maybe four or five hours a day and that was it. And it was like maybe three days, four days possibly." Nor did he see any skulduggery that would indicate that the group were not in possession of the necessary papers to be recording in a foreign country. "Everything was clear and above board and nice," he says. "They said they were going to be there at a certain time, they showed up and had a good time."

In fact, far from any panic at the fact that they had to finish the record before the week was up, the Stones decided to jettison the version(s) of "Country Honk" recorded at Olympic and to remake it from scratch. This version would feature fiddle-playing by one Byron Berline. "I got Byron Berline and all the country musicians for them," says Botnick. "We brought in Byron Berline and a few other country guys that were in L.A. and I believe Keith played with them. It was nice. It was a very quick date, very quick session." Apart from co-writing and singing it, Jagger's other contribution to the track was the beep heard at the start. "We took a stereo microphone and put it out in the street and Mick went outside and honked the horn on the car," Botnick explains.

Meanwhile, saxophonist Bobby Keyes was brought in to add a last bit of raunchy sweetening to "Live With Me". Botnick explains, "I brought Bobby in from Delaney and Bonnie. He's a very sweet man. He's a really fine saxophonist. They were aware of Delaney and Bonnie. David Anderley had signed them and they had produced them, so they were aware. They may have said to David, they may have said to me, 'What about this saxophone player?' and got on the phone and got him." Bobby Keyes later commented, "Both the horns and Mick Taylor made their debut on the same album on the same track. At the time a lot of people overlooked the fact that it wasn't just Mick [Taylor] joining the band, that was the whole period where the horns joined too. And they all left at the same time." The sleevenotes stated that the horns on "Live With Me" were arranged by Leon Russell, who of course had also played piano on it. As Russell laid down his part at Olympic, this might mean that Keyes' sax work actually replaced a previous Russell-orchestrated horn part.

Meanwhile, the sweetening—if such a gritty, even elemental contribution can be termed such—applied to "Gimme Shelter" was stunning. "Mick asked if I knew a singer and I suggested Merry Clayton," says Botnick. "I'd been working with her husband, a saxophonist, Curtis Amy, and I knew Merry through Jack Nitzsche. Merry used to sing background vocals. She came in and they were all very sweet and charming to one another and she enjoyed the song, as you can tell, and gave a great performance." Clayton's impassioned voice can be heard in unison with Jagger through most of the song and—triumphantly—on its own in the middle section (the refrain "Rape, murder! It's just a shot away"). Though no doubt "Gimme Shelter" would still be a timeless track without it, Clayton's input helped seal its classic status. As George Chkiantz puts it, "When the tape came back with that on it, I thought, 'Yeah!' And still do." Asked how many takes did Clayton need for her hair-raising performance, Botnick says, "Not many. Maybe two." Incidentally, the interaction with Clayton may not have been quite as "nice" as Botnick remembers. Other witnesses recall the freshly arrived Clayton going up to Jagger and saying, "Man, I thought you was a man but you nothing but a skinny little boy!" There was also the unfortunate matter of Clayton, having rendered the first chorus to everybody's satisfaction, electing to decline to sing further until her fee was settled to her satisfaction.

For Keith Richards, the finished track was one of the only times in his career (part of "Jumpin' Jack Flash" is the only other example) where what he originally heard in his head was how the song sounded when translated to tape. Speaking to *Uncut* magazine in 2002, he said, "Usually when you write a song, by the time you've recorded it and it's gone through the whole process, it's changed its course for one reason or another, usually for the better ... You write a song and then think, 'Let's see what the other guys think.' Because that's really part of the magic. You come up with an idea and you pass it though the rest of the band and it's what the band does with it that makes the magic." Not this time. "It sounded like what I was hearing in my head as I was writing it."

Botnick is also adamant that no recording could have been done at Sunset Sounds—or anywhere else—after the band had finished in Elektra. "We redid mixing, did all the vocals overdubs with Mick that he hadn't done and assembled it and then took it over to Bob McCloud at Artists And Sounds and mastered the album there for them," he recalls. "This happened right away. They were starting their tour. The minute we finished recording, they were [playing] at the Forum, with Ike and Tina Turner. I remember going to the concert. Maybe like a day later, something like that."

The Stones had originally wanted a work by the surreal artist M.C. Escher to grace the cover of their new album. Escher specialized in visual games involving impossible perspectives, and in what he called *Metamorphosis*, whereby one object changed into another. Jagger sent Escher a letter in January '69 telling him he found his style "quite incredible" and asking him if he would be interested in either designing a picture or providing an unpublished work for the cover of the band's next album (which he was then optimistically thinking would be released in March or April). If Jagger was assuming from Escher's unconventional style that he would be a kindred spirit, he was in for a rude shock. A few days later, Escher responded with a rather tart and starchy note in which he declined the offer due to other commitments and took umbrage that Jagger had presumed to address him by his first name in his missive. (Presumably, another approach by the representatives of the band Mott The Hoople was more polite in Escher's eyes, for he allowed them to use one of his pictures on their eponymous debut album the following year.)

As it turned out, *Let It Bleed* would feature one of the most memorable album sleeves in rock history, even if it wasn't to everyone's taste. Its front cover was occupied almost completely by a picture of a rather bizarre cake. The cake's top layer was a conventional and prettily decorated—including by five miniature Rolling Stones—iced sponge. Its next layer was a bicycle tire. Beneath that was a pizza. A clock face sat beneath the pizza. The next layer was a tape canister with a piece of red tape affixed to it on which was scrawled "STONES—LET IT BLEED." Beneath that was a plate. All of these layers were impaled on an extra-long record-player spindle at the bottom of which sat a vinyl album that bore the name of the artists and the album plus miniature pictures of the Stones' heads. The stylus of what looked like a very old gramophone player was perched on the vinyl. The back cover depicted the same cake but in a rather distressed state. The spindle was bent. The five miniature Stones were scattered or sunk into the sponge cake, out of which a slice had been cut. The tire was torn, punctured, and bandaged. A slice was missing from the pizza. The clock face had been disfigured. The tape canister was broken and spools of tape hung from it. Down at the bottom, the vinyl record was smashed and littered with a pizza slice, shards of plate, pieces of cake, and the detached gramophone arm.

This whole concoction was the work of the late American graphic designer Robert Brownjohn. Brownjohn was well known in his field. It was he who had come up with the idea of projecting the credits of the Bond movie *From Russia With Love* onto a female torso and of promoting another Bond flick, *Goldfinger,* with a naked blonde girl in reference to the grisly death of a character in the film. He presented sketches of the album cover idea to Keith Richards on August 21. The guitarist liked the idea. Bill Wyman reports in *Rolling With The Stones* that the album didn't have a title at this point but one in contention was *Automatic Changer*, a reference to the function that some record players had in those days of playing a series of discs stacked on its spindle one after the other. It's not known whether Brownjohn designed the cake after being told the title or whether the title followed the creation of the cake. Another working title for the album—and Keith's preferred choice—was *Hard Knox And Durty Sox*. The photograph of the cake was taken by Don McAllester.

In a scarcely credible twist of fate, the sponge layer of the cake on the cover of this utterly decadent album was baked by Delia Smith. Smith is now a household name—at least to British audiences—as a T.V. chef and author (one of her cookery books was one of the fastest-selling tomes in history) and is the epitome of clean-cut. At the time, she was less well known, working for a food photographer, but had started her own column in the compact *Daily Mirror*. "One day they said they wanted a cake for a Rolling Stones record cover," she said later. "It was another job at the time. They wanted it to be very over the top and as gaudy as I could make it." Chkiantz recalls, "She was shacking up with a bloke who was staying at a friend of mine's apartment. Neither of them had a clue how to cook and it was this friend of mine who told them how to cook a sponge cake. She was too busy to do anything very much else." It's not known how much of Brownjohn's £1,000 budget was spent on Smith's cake.

The actual assembling of the sleeve and inner sleeve was done by Victor Kahn, a 26-year-old New York graphic artist who designed album packaging for Alan Steckler, who was the graphics vice president for A.B.K.C.O., Allen Klein's management company. "My first Stones involvement was *Through The Past Darkly (Big Hits Vol 2)*, which was the strange octagon-shaped album," Kahn recalls. "Sure, cutting off the corners on the album was a great idea, but it was really more about updating album sound reproduction and content on a compilation which contained the first stereo releases of songs like "Honky Tonk Women", "Ruby Tuesday", and "Jumpin' Jack Flash".

"Releases in stereo were very important in those days ... A year later I designed the 'Hey Jude' [Beatles] cover for A.B.K.C.O., forcing them to name it that because of the first stereo release of the song 'Hey Jude" They had already pressed (but not released) one million L.P. records with the name *Beatles Again* on the Apple label, but it was at my insistence that the album name was changed because of the long-awaited stereo mix of what is now the greatest Beatles song of all time in stereo. The whole stereo thing opened doors to the next album I designed for the Stones." Kahn is referring to *The Rolling Stones: A Special Radio Promotion Album In Limited Edition*, an album pressed for US radio stations in October 1969 which featured an array of their greatest hits but also a preview of "Love In Vain" from the still-to-be-released *Let It Bleed*. (Contrary to myth, this version of "Love In Vain" is not different to the one on *Let It Bleed*.)

By the time Brownjohn had finished his cake, the title had evidently been changed, because the photographs that Kahn worked with already had the *Let It Bleed* title on the canister and the vinyl L.P. label. This title change scrambled the meaning of the items stacked for play on the spindle. For his part, Kahn says, "The name *Automatic Changer* never reached me or anybody that I knew in the New York office."

"The original photo that I cropped the cover image from even went as far as having a ball of clay holding the old gramophone record arm and needle that you see part of in the picture," says Kahn. "This was kind of a long faraway picture of a table with a nice piece of paper over it and the whole cake and record player thing standing and a piece of clay holding up the old broken record arm." He continues, "What a wonderful opportunity that I was given to assemble the package and write the words for the liner sleeve and do the poster. I chose to credit the artists on the recording sessions that went beyond just the Stones playing the instruments. A first in artist credits for a Rolling Stones album and a first in album detail that has now stood the test of time." Unfortunately, the credit list that Kahn was given contained more than one error: Nanette Workman is referred to as Nanette Newman (the name of an English actress even more white-bread than Delia Smith) and the line "George Chkiantz Alias Irish O'Duffy" in the "Boys In The Back Room" actually conflated two people. "Irish" was actually Alan O'Duffy, a remnant of his days at Pye Studios where there were three engineers called Alan and nicknames therefore required to avoid confusion. "Don't know how Irish felt (I never asked him)," says Chkiantz. "I was irritated, but I thought that someone had done it to wind us up so I kept quiet." O'Duffy says he was "well annoyed, then I just thought the person doing the credits on the album was stoned as well! Couldn't get their act together. Amused as well, as we do not look at all alike!" In addition, only one non-Stone instrumentalist was credited on "Country Honk", an error if we are to accept Bruce Botnick's recollection that more than one country musician was recruited for the remake at Elektra.

Kahn was also instructed to insert the phrase "Hard Knox and Durty Sox" atop the credits. "It never dawned on me that that could have been a working title for the album," he now says. He was also instructed to credit the writing of "Love In Vain" to "Woody Payne'" This was the pseudonym of an unknown individual who claimed copyright on all Johnson songs, knowing there was no heir. Kahn adds, "I personally wrote the line at the end in caps, 'THIS RECORD SHOULD BE PLAYED LOUD.' I guess because I heard it in vinyl mixdown for the pressing of the record and it was incredible and it was so loud in the studio, the line just came to me."

The title of the album actually features three times on the front cover: on the canister, the vinyl L.P. label, andt at the top of the sleeve. Kahn says "I would assume that it was the record companies who forced that because of when you're flipping through L.P.s you want to be able to immediately see the name of the artist and the album right at the top. I was definitely instructed for the London logos to go on the top right. To tell you the truth, at the time it was a very common thing to do. The way that things are done now I would say that probably it would have looked better without that being up there altogether and maybe the London logo on the bottom right."

On the back cover, the track titles are printed in a different order to the record, but Kahn says this is for aesthetic reasons. "I [did] it that way to get the right- and left-hand margins perfectly even. Just [to show] the songs on there, not necessarily the order, because I put the correct order on the inner sleeve."

Given away with the album was a poster, also designed by Kahn. "Someone got me a shot of the new five together at that [Hyde Park] concert and I stripped all of them out of that image and dropped it on top of an old great never-published picture of Mick Jagger that I had."

By the time *Let It Bleed* was released, the Stones had made headlines for all the wrong reasons again. Apparently stung by the criticisms of high ticket prices made by the American press—led by *Rolling Stone*—into giving a free concert to climax their U.S. tour, they played to a huge crowd at the Altamont Speedway, California, on December 6. They may have been expecting this to be a blissful occasion like the festivals at Monterey (1967) and Woodstock (earlier in 1969). They may also have been expecting the Hell's Angels employed to police the gig to be the relative pussycats the British Hell's Angels who policed the Hyde Park gig had been. They were wrong on both counts. The whole event was fractious where it wasn't menacing. The Hell's Angels were doling out random violence to crowd members all day long. Mick Jagger got punched in the face by a presumably drug-crazed fan as soon as he stepped off the helicopter transporting the band in. To many who caught the bad vibes there it was shocking but not surprising that a young black man with a white girlfriend called Meredith Hunter was stabbed to death in front of the stage by the Angels while the Stones were performing. Three other people died— as did, for many, the dream of the flower-strewn Sixties proving that mankind could make a better world for itself.

Let It Bleed was released on December 5 1969 in the U.K. and the following day in the U.S. It went to number one in the U.K. and number three in the States.

aftermath

In assembling *Let It Bleed*, the Rolling Stones made some strange decisions about the track listing, decisions which—incredible as it might be for some—made the album weaker than it could have been.

For the record, the album that was to have been titled *Sticky Fingers* and released in September 1969 was planned to comprise (in this sequence): "Midnight Rambler", "Love In Vain", "Let It Bleed", "Monkey Man", "Give Me Some Shelter" (sic), "You Got Some Silver Now" (sic), "Sister Morphine", and "Loving Cup." "Sister Morphine", of course, was one of the outstanding slowies on *Sticky Fingers* and the presence on that album's version of Ry Cooder—who would never work with the Stones again after 1969—indicates that the track must have already been akin to the released version. Only possible complications with the credit due to Marianne Faithfull would seem to account for the decision to consign this to the vaults in favor of weaker fare: when the track appeared on *Fingers*, Jagger and Richards instructed Allen Klein to make sure she got a share of the publishing but not to put her name on the label for fear that royalties would end up with her estranged manager Gerry Bron. "Loving Cup"—a song consigned to the vaults for a year longer than "Sister Morphine", although when it emerged it was as a new recording—would also have made a fine alternative to some of the tracks, especially lyrically, its tenderness and good-natured horniness preferable to the stream-of-consciousness, self-conscious decadence of large parts of the record.

It's possible that Richards—because of its painful associations—would never have countenanced the inclusion of "Memo From Turner" on *Let It Bleed*, so the exclusion of that fine song is understandable. As is the omission of the single that the sessions spawned. Had the album been released two years later, "Honky Tonk Women" would have appeared on it (just as "Brown Sugar" appeared on the *Sticky Fingers* album it heralded in 1971), but at the time it was not yet acceptable to the rock consumer that the rock aristocracy only issue singles to promote a parent album.

There are some other tracks from the period that could arguably have displaced the lesser tracks. "Jiving Sister Fanny", though underdeveloped, would have been preferable to "Love In Vain". "I Don't Know Why", never released on a "proper" Stones album, would also have been a powerful cut on *Let It Bleed*, although some might suggest the inclusion of a cover would detract from the band's own personal imprimatur. A track called "I Don't Know The Reason Why" (not to be confused with "I Don't Know Why") is also reputed to have been recorded during the *Let It Bleed* sessions. However, it's not mentioned in the main text of this book because of doubts about its vintage. Most reference books state that it was probably recorded at Elektra Studios prior to the Stones' '69 U.S. tour, but comments by Bruce Botnick would seem to refute this. It's a sensual 12-bar blues, done electrically and with some telling guitar work from Taylor in the instrumental break. Although overlong, if it does date from the *Let It Bleed* sessions it would have made a preferable inclusion on the album to the other (acoustic) blues, "Love In Vain".

In any case, history can't be undone, and the discussion must center on the songs that were included on the album ...

Gimme Shelter

The music of Led Zeppelin has often been described as "cosmic blues"—that is, a hugely magnified, space-age version of 12-bar blues and rhythm and blues. That description also perfectly describes "Gimme Shelter", which, as it happens, knocks anything Zeppelin did into a cocked hat. And come to that anything done by the Rolling Stones.

The track opens with Keith Richards tiptoeing his way into the song via electric guitar picking so tentative as to be barely audible, like a man gingerly entering a dark and forbidding zone holding unknown terrors. This is appropriate, considering the song's apocalyptic ambience. A guiro or "scraper"—resembling the seconds ticking down to doomsday—begins sounding while subtle drum work enters the picture. The build-up in this introduction is flawless. With each coiling progression of Richards's guitar, a new element is introduced: eerie, cooing female backing vocals, a second guitar line coiling around the first, some slow, dark piano—all these elements creating the assumption in the listener that disaster is just around the bend. Abruptly, with a skitter of drums, the pace quickens and with a lurching movement we are entering the fires of hell, heralded by the way the end of a Richards guitar line suddenly—courtesy of induced amplifier distortion—erupts into flame.

Jagger appears, declaring that a storm is threatening his very life, that shelter is urgently needed, and that if it is not found, he will—in an allusion, maybe unconscious, to one of the

Stones' early hits—"fade away". Merry Clayton—more banshee than soul diva but exquisite nonetheless—joins him on the chorus to holler that "War, children, it's just a shot away!" A second verse of similar foreboding takes place, this time conjuring images of fire sweeping the streets. Another hollered chorus sweeps us into what is one of the most extraordinary instrumental breaks in rock history, inaugurated by a typical adroitly judged Watts cymbal splash. Across this soundscape comes a blast of mouth harp that is so colossal that it sounds like the instrument belongs to the very gods that the narrator is implicitly beseeching. The harp's brutal, metallic rasping blasts back and forth for several seconds before Richards takes over with some similarly larger-than-life guitar work.

Jagger is heard briefly and incoherently bellowing in the background, and it sounds like a cry of encouragement to Clayton, for now it is she on her own who takes charge, declaring over and over again:

Rape, murder!

It's just a shot away!

It's just a shot away!

Another blast of gargantuan mouth harp and Jagger takes center-stage once more to enunciate the third verse, this one fearful of torrential floods. The final verse, though, is an optimistic one, suggesting that love is just a kiss away, and on that thought the musical elements that have exhibited sustained brilliance throughout—the sizzling guitars, the wailing mouth harp, the muscular drumming, the rattling piano, the sonic juggernaut that is the sum of all those things—take us into a fade.

"Gimme Shelter" is a titanic performance by everyone concerned, one of those tracks that reward concentration with unalloyed joy because the listener cannot pinpoint a single moment that is not compelling. In other words, perfection.

Love In Vain

It would be difficult for any track to follow that titanic accomplishment, but it has to be said that the dramatic opening of *Let It Bleed* is followed by something of a longueur. "Love In Vain" and "Country Honk" are a couple of tracks that don't quite come off.

The chief blame for the aesthetic failure of "Love In Vain" must lie with Mick Jagger. His vocal performance on the Stones' first-ever released Robert Johnson cover seems to be an attempt to cross the studiedly indolent (a manner whose projection in the Sixties had socio-political implications unimaginable today) with the authentically down-home. The result is appalling, his microphone work more like braying than singing. This is a pity, for in other areas the band imaginatively opt to open out what had been a straightforward and spartan 12-bar blues number. The opening acoustic guitar figure is lovely, as is the general air of vulnerability. Somehow, though, the track overall does not gel, never sounding like more than the sum of its constituent parts, some of which, like Watts's thudding drums, are jarringly inappropriate. Cooder's mandolin solo, meanwhile, doesn't quite provide the sweeping lift it's supposed to.

Country Honk

John Lennon used to taunt the Stones for doing things six months after The Beatles did. This shadowing seems to inform the decision to include an acoustic version of "Honky Tonk Women" on *Let It Bleed* the year after The Beatles put on an album (The Beatles) an acoustic version of a rock track that had appeared on a single ("Revolution").

As with that latter number, it's difficult to gauge how we would perceive it had we never heard the electric version. Even though in both cases the acoustic arrangement to some extent preceded the electric rendition, it can't help but sound like a parody of the more familiar electric arrangement, a quaint piss-take not far off from Peter Sellers' Shakespearean rendition of "A Hard Day's Night". However, even the steeliest determination to approach the acoustic "Revolution 1" with an open mind yields nothing other than the feeling that that track is boring and suffocating. The same can't be said for "Country Honk", but neither is it a classic.

The strummed acoustic guitar figure that opens proceedings is attention-grabbingly sharp and attractive. Mick's singing is nicely underplayed, him singing the "Give me give me give me the honky tonk blues" tag-line with precisely the understatement this arrangement merits, just as the single version's hip-grinding ambience called for the yowling treatment he gave it in that. The second verse of the song is the same as in its rock antecedent, but the sharp first verse sees a relocation from Memphis to Jackson, where the protagonist is not consorting with gin-soaked bar-room queens but "Sittin' in a bar tippling a jar."

Ironically, the fiddle part the band added at the last minute at Elektra is the track's undoing. Though Berline was clearly talented on his instrument, the part he plays is whining and intrusive. The recording that exists *sans* fiddle is far superior, boasting a two-acoustic-guitar harmony part in the middle and more audible flecks of pedal steel.

Live With Me

At the start of this song, Jagger unleashes an affected semi-sniff, semi-yawn, a yobbish gesture one would expect from someone in his early teenage years who wanted to shock his elders. This sets the tone for the track, a raucous and self-conscious rejection of middle-class mores. The narrator starts off with the boast "I got nasty habits," a strange opening gambit for an individual trying to persuade the object of his desires to share the same roof. If it's an attempt to project the cool rebelliousness so in vogue in the decade of its making, it's slightly undermined by the credentials the narrator then uses to back up his claim, "I take tea at three." You radical! But then, maybe that sums Mick Jagger up. His rebelliousness has never been a matter of manning the barricades but of living life as he wants to, rather than the way that people who consider themselves his elders or betters think is right. Not that the fact that he is a libertarian rather than a revolutionary diminishes him—never let it be forgotten that he paid the price for being seen as a figurehead for those who wanted a fairer, freer society by being hounded by the authorities and by getting a prison sentence—but the fact that he was no political activist may explain the vacuousness at the heart of the lyric of "Live With Me". In it, he brags that the meat he eats for dinner must be hung up for a week, his best friend shoots water rats, he has a score of dirty, music-obsessed children locked in the nursery, and house staff who second as whores, strippers, and lechers. To many of the generation who came of age with him or slightly behind him, such piling on of outrageous imagery must have been delicious.

After all, it was only a few years earlier that the presence of such things in a mainstream pop record would have been unthinkable: the media was in the grip of those who frowned on mention of carnal activities (especially outside marriage) and unconventional behavior, leading to a preposterously bland portrayal of the world in which their readers/viewers/listeners lived. It must have been truly heady for the young and/or unconventional to now find their life, language, and attitudes reflected instead of hidden by the music to which they listened and therefore the media on which it was broadcast. Today, obscenity, ostentatious unconventional behavior, and hedonistic values are to be seen—in many cases celebrated—in the media every day. In such a context, the lyric of a song like "Live With Me" cannot have the same import it did, especially to new generations of listeners. Once these lyrics are removed from the times to which they were a reaction, what is left? Well, unfortunately not much more than a litany of smut, a sort of grittier "My Ding-A-Ling".

However, the track is redeemed by its rock 'n' roll vitality. A burbling, slightly sinister bass run begins proceedings, followed by some brisk drumming that heralds a marching tempo. After the first verse, a glissando from Russell or Hopkins heralds a move up a notch or two in beefiness. The thumping piano track is joined at the end of the second verse by saxophone before Keyes is given the spotlight for the solo, which he tackles gamely while Charlie provides cymbal splashes galore in the background. It's Charlie in fact who goes into overdrive at the end, bass pedal and cymbal working constantly as he ups the tempo to take the song into the fade. Not the greatest of Stones rockers—there's something slightly too forced for that—but a perfectly diverting few minutes.

Let It Bleed

A sort of elongated, downbeat version of the preceding track, once again we find Jagger in lascivious and mischievous mode. It's difficult to assess whether the title of the song (which doesn't occur in the lyric) was a nod to The Beatles' song "Let It Be". Although the Fab Four's track would not be released until early 1970, the two bands, of course, shared the same management and were friends, so the Stones could easily have heard of the Beatles title well before release, not least because it was first recorded as far back as January '69. Interestingly, the two songs highlight the differences between the groups: whereas "Let It Be" was almost the apotheosis of The Beatles' perennial optimism and tenderness, "Let It Bleed" showed the Stones in all their decadent, amoral glory. If indeed glory is the right word for a track whose lyric seems a stream of consciousness whose one constant theme is a desire to shock for the sake of it.

Jagger opens with an innocuous verse in which he offers to be the someone to lean on to the person at whom the song is directed. By the second verse, he has managed to work in a mention of the addressee's breasts, an allusion to her genitals (parking lot), and cocaine. The repetition of the chorus, meanwhile, sees "lean on me" change to "cream on me." The middle-eight sees the hoped-for engagement of the narrator scuppered by the woman's decision to stab him in his basement (which we are told in irrelevant detail is "dirty filthy") in the company of a junkie nurse. "Oh what pleasant company!" says Jagger before a new chorus where "cream on" becomes "feed on" to reflect that the situation has now descended into cannibalism, Jagger imploring, "Take my arm, take my leg, oh baby don't you take my head." The final verse features the "We all need someone we can bleed on/And if you want it, baby, well you can bleed on me" line that appears to give the track its title.

This lyric is clearly pure garbage, a succession of what Jagger imagines are clever phrases and audacious rhymes, painfully self-conscious imagery and a narrative progression based on authorial whim. Though Jagger invests passion in singing it, it communicates nothing, nor does it attempt to: no moral, message or idea. It merely occupies space—and slightly disagreeably so. Like "Live With Me", the whole thing is a now dated exercise in living up to a public image of the Rolling Stones. The only hope for this track resides with the musical accompaniment, and it is here that the Stones prove their mettle. Only a great band can turn garbage into a highly listenable experience, and this is what the Stones do here. Providing the song's background is Ian Stewart's irrepressibly bubbling piano and Charlie's muscular drumming. The mid-tempo music has the relaxed and loose feel of a jam, but is clearly well rehearsed, with carefully incremental layering. There are also a couple of nice, exotic background decorations at the beginning, one of which sounds like beans being turned in a drum, the other like distant R.K.O. radio signals. After a while, it is Keith's cawing, keening electric guitar that dominates proceedings. The fade-out sees some nice extemporizing, with Charlie reeling off drum flourishes and Jagger semi-scat singing, including some call-and-response with Keith's guitar lines. All of this salvages what would be an utterly lightweight number, but one can't but be left with the impression that the first-ever song that gave a Stones album its title in no way deserves that status.

Midnight Rambler

One really doesn't want to belabor the point about the way societal changes—some of which the Stones are responsible for—have dated parts of *Let It Bleed*. However, it must be noted that whatever its qualities, "Midnight Rambler" has a grisly side. Essentially, it glorifies a rapist. It is based loosely on the case of the Sixties mass murderer the Boston Strangler, although it also carries the line, "You heard about the Boston [pause], well, honey, it's not one of those ...." In 1969, such were the headily anti-conventional times that nobody really thought to question deriving outlaw chic from such a subject matter. In addition, one wonders whether the modern-day Jagger—now the father of several daughters—would even countenance writing a number that ends with the line "I'll stick my knife right down your throat baby and it hurts."

Musically, however, "Midnight Rambler" is impeccable. It is an example of how an atmosphere can be evoked with the most basic rock set-up—if you are a band of the caliber of the Rolling Stones. This slinky, menacing, lengthy creation (at just shy of seven minutes, the second-longest track on the album) is comprised mainly of just one electric guitar, bass, drums, and mouth harp. While on "You Can't Always Get What You Want" and to an extent "Gimme Shelter," the Stones drive home the message of the song's lyric with sumptuous accompaniments and detailed production, on "Midnight Rambler" they prove their origins as a gutsy rhythm and blues band and the values learned from them are not forgotten. Despite the bare-bones set-up, the track in no way feels underdressed or lackluster.

Although such sparse instrumentation doesn't lend itself much to production tricks, there are little tweaks and flourishes that make vital differences, starting with the way Richards's guitar is treated to sound like he's playing in some dank, concrete chamber rather than a warm, carpeted studio. The same goes for Jagger's blaring mouth harp, which through most of the song marches in menacing tandem with Keith's ebbing and flowing razor-sharp lines. In one particularly galvanizing section during the instrumental break, they quicken the listener's pulse by upping the tempo, Mick huffing furiously away while his voice repeatedly intones "Don't you do that" as Keith and Charlie pound away in brutal synchronism. It engenders a sinister musical strut. Some prefer the live version of "Midnight Rambler" heard on the souvenir of their '69 American tour *Get Yer Ya-Yas Out* for the way it dramatically emphasizes the swells and sudden stops in the song, but that rendition has a tinniness common in so many live recordings of the era, a quality a world removed from the dark, supple grace of the *Let It Bleed* original.

"Midnight Rambler" has a lyric sections of which make one wince or wish to blot them out, but overall it is like a modern-day equivalent and extrapolation of a Robert Johnson haunted blues number, a thoroughly spooky and shadowy creation.

You Got The Silver

If there could possibly be a positive result from Jagger's dalliance with Anita Pallenberg on the set of *Performance*, it stems from the fact that it produced some great songs. Not just in the shape of "Gimme Shelter" but in this beautiful plaintive ballad.

Though Jagger's attempt at a vocal on this song was technically competent and soulful, it's good that Richards's vocal take was ultimately chosen for the album, for the introduction of his voice adds a different timbre and therefore another variety of tone.

The first couple of verses are musically almost rustic. Richards's declaration that his love has got the qualities of silver, gold, and diamonds—as well as the possession of his heart and soul—are set against his voice, his twanging acoustic guitar, glimmers of pedal steel and his cawing electric guitar overdubs. After the first chorus, though, Nicky Hopkins' organ tiptoes in (as though not wanting to intrude on the gentle mood) to add a sheen to the proceedings. With the third verse (a repetition of the first), the mood changes. There's a jolt into a faster tempo, Charlie begins energetic drumming, and Hopkins' piano begins thumping (though discreetly mixed back). Keith sings the rest of the song in impassioned tones, as though tired of the politeness displayed at the beginning of the song. Now Keith is demanding, "What's that laughing in your smile?" It sounds like a man afraid that his lover is mocking him, and there is a hint of denial when he insists about this, "I don't care, no, I don't care!" The fact that he doesn't care—or is trying to convince himself he doesn't care—is underpinned by the finale, which is partly a repetition of the chorus in which he compares his lover to the earth's precious metals but ends—Richards's voice by now almost a yell—with the couplet, "Your love, just leave me blind/I don't care, no, that's the big surprise."

It certainly sounds like the ballad of a torn man, who knows his relationship is not the ideal scene he wants it to be but who nonetheless receives such joy from it that he dare not rock the boat. Ring a bell? Perhaps it's unwise to read too much into lyrics. After all, even if we knew nothing about the Mick/Keith/Anita triangle that seems to have inspired it, "You Got The Silver" would still be a beautiful and moving love song.

Monkey Man

George Chkiantz may have initially disliked "Monkey Man" for its unStonesy production, but it's that very polish—sort of a cinema soundtrack glossiness—that helps *Let It Bleed* achieve greatness. No classic album ever had a monotone. It is not just technical proficiency and inspired songwriting that make a great L.P., but an additional ingredient of variety of mood, texture, and tempo, a breadth and reach that dazzle the listener. Even an album like The Clash's eponymous debut—though it was recorded in a minimalist style—actually takes in several different atmospheres and shades. If the Stones had put out an album which had nine different variations of either "Midnight Rambler" or "Monkey Man", it would have made for a highly listenable experience to be sure, but not a classic one. It is the very fact that a piece of spiky, minimalist menace like "Midnight Rambler" could inhabit the same album as an exercise in musical elegance and high production values such as "Monkey Man" that places *Let It Bleed* in the album hall of fame.

Right from the off, "Monkey Man" has an airbrushed and darkly atmospheric tone. Wyman plays short, twinkling glissandos on the vibes while instruments hum into life behind him. A cluster of spiky guitar notes cues Jagger to start enunciating his lyric, which is basically a continuation—or let's say repetition—of the "I'm very decadent, please be my bed partner" message of "Live With Me". At times he seems to approach candor, as in the line "All my friends are junkies, well that's not really true," possibly a reference to Faithfull and Richards, the two people closest to him in his life, both dabbing in heroin. "Well, I hope we're not too messianic/Or a trifle too satanic/We love to play the blues"—these lines hardly need explaining in their reference to the band's public image. (Things were going to get worse here: the events of Altamont would confirm the demonic aura some of the public saw around the Stones.) However, when he then goes on to declare, "I've been bit and I've been tossed around/By every she-rat in this town," this seems to bear no relation to any facts we know about Jagger's life. It could be that he was so disappointed by the traumas of his relationships with Shrimpton and Faithfull (again, with her overdose, the latter soon to get far worse) that this genuinely was his point of view, but somehow the song doesn't have the smack of the autobiographical or confessional but rather of Jagger adhering to the man-done-wrong conventions of blues and rock songwriting. It's not as if Jagger can't do confessional: *Exile On Main Street* was littered with references to his then wife's pregnancy and his feelings on becoming a father, while *Primitive Cool*, his much underrated 1987 solo album, spoke frankly about memories of postwar austerity and his feelings about growing old. Often, though, he does what he does here and adopts the role of the cartoon Jagger: affectedly obnoxious and artless.

The musical backdrop against which he does this is anything but artless. In fact, this is some of the artiest, most sophisticated music to which the Stones ever attached their names. The song's centerpiece is an extraordinarily lengthy—for them—instrumental break of a quite magisterial and sweeping quality. During this near one-and-a-half minutes, Charlie is playing almost timpani-like drum parts and we hear several varieties of guitar style from Keith overlaid atop each other—a crow's-call sound, a lengthy semi-flamenco electric guitar run, and the deep, resonating noise of the pedal steel. Richards also plays alongside lovely long descending Hopkins piano progressions for several exquisite bars. In addition, there is more of that twinkling vibraphone.

When Jagger comes back in, he is virtually retching his nonsensical title phrases—like a monkey, in fact—but this contrast between the sublime and the ridiculous doesn't detract from the graceful power of the track.

You Can't Always Get What You Want

The angelic voices of the London Bach Choir sing the first verse of *Let It Bleed*'s finale unaccompanied by any musical instrument. The aura of virginal innocence is soon dispelled in a tale of dissolution and disillusion, although the blow is softened by some utterly lovely music.

The first piece of loveliness is Keith's opening sweet little acoustic guitar figure, which is almost immediately joined by a French horn part from Kooper that is no less gorgeous for its haunting melancholy. Cue Jagger singing unaffectedly and convincingly a first verse that depicts a drug-addled woman and her downtrodden lover (presumably Faithfull and Jagger respectively—as Faithfull is on record as believing). "You can't always get what you want," Jagger then intones three times, before qualifying the despondency with "But if you try sometimes, you get what you need." As he does so, Kooper provides a dramatic, airy sweep on the piano keys and the track's percussive backbone kicks in, helped along by rumbling piano. The second verse sees Jagger referring to a street demo, possibly a London protest against the Vietnam war in July 1968 which he attended. The protesters talk of blowing a fuse if they don't vent their frustration—cue the repetitions of the philosophical chorus. By now, Jagger is joined on the choruses by the gravely throats of Nanette Workman and Madeline Bell. After the second verse—like the first, ends with a dramatic female voice singing the last line with Jagger in tandem—we are into an extended third verse that serves as a middle section. To the background of a zigzagging organ and rattling tabla, Jagger speaks of running into a friend called Mr. Jimmy at the Chelsea drugstore—a real place, but Jagger is possibly using it as a metaphor for a drug-dealer's lair. Mr. Jimmy is possibly Jimi Hendrix, who was then known to be sinking further into hard drugs. The instrumental break is heralded by more sweeping piano work from Kooper and sees the London Bach Choir coo half-soothingly, half-ominously in the background.

The drug-addled woman returns for the last verse. Her partner is now not merely downtrodden but bleeding. Jagger sings the chorus one last time. This is followed by an instrumental passage/fade-out that is quite a ride: sweeping, blurred-fingered keyboards from Kooper, swelling choral parts from the choir, pulsating tabla, and double-time drumming.

The true test of a track of epic length is whether it retains its air of grandiosity for the listener without being patience-wearing. It's a test that "You Can't Always Get What You Want" passes triumphantly. Its seven-and-a-half minutes simply fly by, in truth far quicker than does The Beatles' "Hey Jude'" the track to which it has been compared so many times, which starts beautifully but fails to hold the attention in the final furlong. The track is not the masterpiece that perhaps it was intended to be. Sometimes simplicity and visceral excitement can work more effectively than endless run-throughs, overdubs, and ornamentation (witness the primeval brilliance of "'Satisfaction"). Nonetheless, "You Can't Always Get What You Want" is a blissful listening experience and utter proof—back in the days when such proof was needed—that rock music could constitute high art.

Overview

Let It Bleed is a great Stones album but not their best.

It is the least of the quartet of four studio albums from the era 1968–1972 that are considered their meisterwerks: *Beggars Banquet, Let It Bleed, Sticky Fingers,* and *Exile On Main Street.* There is merit in rejecting *Let It Bleed* in favor of any of those albums (just as there is in opting for three other great if neglected Stones albums as their finest long-playing moment: *The Rolling Stones* (1964), *Aftermath* (1966), and 1978's *Some Girls*). *Beggars Banquet* has a unique acoustic ambience and bluesiness and dense, sinewy textures that seem to hold more gravitas than *Let It Bleed*'s superficial flash. *Sticky Fingers* exults in the same decadence as *Let It Bleed*, but more thoughtfully. *Exile On Main Street* has the sweep and the variety granted by a double album's playing time and therefore the feel of a grand statement and magnum opus. However, weighing heavily in *Let It Bleed*'s favor is the presence on it of those two titanic classics that top and tail it, "Gimme Shelter" and "You Can't Always Get What You Want". No matter how good any of the other albums mentioned, none of them can boast anything quite as powerful.

True, *Let It Bleed*'s lyrics are in most places inferior to those on that trio of other albums from the Stones' golden era. In too many places, Jagger is here at his most juvenile and cartoonishly rebellious, and while that rebelliousness had an impact at a time when—to both the outrage and delight of Stones fans—Jagger was public enemy number one, three-and-a-half decades and several musical consumer generations later they carry none of the sociopolitical weight they once did. In some instances—e.g. "Midnight Rambler"—they have dated quite horrifically. Musically, though, the album's power cannot be denied. "Love In Vain" and "Country Honk" are negligible but the playing everywhere else, both by the Stones and by their always adroitly chosen guests, is impeccable. The four songs on the original side two of the vinyl album—"Midnight Rambler", "You Got The Silver", "Monkey Man", and "You Can't Always Get What You Want"—are devastating in their aesthetic brilliance and variety.

Upon its release, Greil Marcus reviewed the album in *Rolling Stone* magazine (named, incidentally, partly after the group: Muddy Waters' song "Rollin' Stone", Bob Dylan's "Like A Rolling Stone", and the proverb that ends in "gathers no moss" were also given as reasons in that magazine's first editorial). In his write-up, he was obsessed—as people tend to be at the close of a decade, especially one as momentous and epoch-marking as the Sixties—with the ending of an era, opening with the observation that this would be the last Stones album of this one. Though he didn't mention Altamont, some of this may have been prompted by the horrified reaction that festival's events induced, as though a bubble of love and hope created by the blissful Monterey and Woodstock gatherings had been popped and reality come crashing in. He was dismissive of the album's packaging—"It has the crummiest cover art since *Flowers*, with a credit sheet that looks like it was designed by the United States Government Printing Office (all courtesy of the inflated Robert Brownjohn)"—but in no way of the album. "Like *Beggars Banquet*, *Let It Bleed* has the feel of *Highway 61 Revisited*", he wrote, comparing it to the 1965 album that many to this day consider Bob Dylan's finest hour. He continued, "On songs like 'Live With Me', 'Midnight Rambler', and 'Let It Bleed', the Stones prance through all their familiar roles, with their Rolling Stones masks on, full of lurking evil, garish sexuality, and the hilarious and exciting posturing of rock 'n' roll Don Juans. On 'Monkey Man' they grandly submit to the image they've carried for almost the whole decade, and then crack up digging it: 'All my friends are junkies! (That's not really true ...)' And there are other songs, hidden between the flashier cuts, waiting for the listener to catch up with them: the brilliant revival of Robert Johnson's exquisite 'Love In Vain', and Keith Richards's haunting ride through the diamond mines, 'You Got The Silver'. And yet it's the first and last of *Let It Bleed* that seem to matter most. The frightening desperation of 'Gimmie Shelter' [sic[and the confused frustration of 'You Can't Always Get What You Want' give the lie to the bravado of 'Midnight Rambler' or 'Live With Me'. Not that those songs don't work—they do, of course, as crunching, soaring dreams of conquest and pop supremacy. They're great numbers. But 'Gimmie Shelter' [sic[and 'You Can't Always Get What You Want' both reach for reality and end up confronting it, almost mastering what's real, or what reality will feel like as the years fade in. It's a long way from 'Get Off My Cloud' to 'Gimmie Shelter' [sic], a long way from 'I Can't Get No Satisfaction' to 'You Can't Always Get What You Want'."

In his concluding paragraph, Marcus said, "So in *Let It Bleed* we can find every role the Stones have ever played for us— swaggering studs, evil demons, harem keepers and fast life riders—what the Stones meant in the Sixties, what they know very well they've meant to us. But at the beginning and the end you'll find an opening into the Seventies—harder to take, and stronger wine." In reference to the gutsy singing of Clayton, who he was surprised to see given the opportunity to hold her own with Jagger, he summed up, "They have women with them this time, and these two magnificent songs no longer reach for mastery over other people, but for an uncertain mastery over the more desperate situations the coming years are about to enforce."

Across the Atlantic, the *New Musical Express* also gave the album a lengthy review. Though it would soon become the British equivalent of *Rolling Stone* in being the preferred journal of the radical and the underground, the tone of the review/track rundown by Richard Green indicated the paper's still lingering puff-piece heritage. "What a great album!" Green began, shooting his bolt. "The Stones have obviously put a lot of thought and hard work into it and I have no hesitation in naming it one of the top five L.P.s of 1969—people are going to have to go a long way to beat it. There's so much variety that each track makes you want to hear it again and again … It's an incredible piece of work that shows the group and friends at their best." "Gimme Shelter" inspired less intellectual and ornate prose than it did from Marcus. "One of the Stones' mid-tempo specialties, with a heavy beat and tons of oomph. Mick sings the first part and is then joined by Keith and Mary [sic] Clayton, before a guitar break that leads into a yelling solo by Mary. The whole thing becomes louder and wilder with Mick on harmonica and the rhythm section letting rip." Mysteriously, he found the title track "a lot like the first track in style." "Ye Gods!" was his response to the extravaganza of "You Can't Always Get What You Want", which he guilelessly described as "A long track full of surprises, and a credit to producer Jimmy Miller and all involved!"

Back across the Atlantic, *The New York Times* carried a review by Don Heckman whose thoughtfulness and willingness to view rock as a valid medium would then have been unimaginable in most British daily newspapers. It actually barely discussed *Let It Bleed* but it is required reading for anyone who wants to know precisely what the Stones meant for their generation. Heckman opened with an expression of shock that rock had now lasted a decade and a half. "Has any other stylistic movement in American popular music ... been so powerful for so long ... And what makes it all the more significant, rock shows little signs of deterioration." Heckman made intelligent points about how until the Sixties nobody had been interested in what the young thought, until their numbers and hence purchasing power made them important. He also put his finger on the nature of what he called their oppression of the spirit, "their intense hatred of a war for which they served (and serve) as cannon fodder, their search for personal relationships free of the encrustation of traditional social hypocrisy, their experiments with their own kind of drugs and stimulants." In that sense, he said, the young white kids were now feeling something akin to what blacks had felt for centuries. The appeal of Mick Jagger to them, he opined, "is the feeling of community, shared ideals, emotions and a common language." In reference to the mentions of sex on *Let It Bleed*—and in response to a recent Albert Goldman article which, referring to the mass, organized movement of people in the form of marches, demos, and festivals that went side by side with popular music at the time, described rock as "Fascism spelled fashion"—he said, "Far from urging his listeners toward mass, mindless conformity, Jagger is calling for the open, uncluttered expression of feelings that young whites have been asked to repress for most of their lives." Finally, he turned his attention fully to the new album, which he said, "presents the Stones in their strongest suit—heavy, black-tinged, passionately erotic hard rock/blues." He concluded, "The

Stones will never make the kind of impact upon the mass market that The Beatles have. It is their fate, I suspect, to remain outside the corridors of middle class preference precisely because their music and their manners represent such an affront to the shibboleths of white respectability. But it is probably also true that the rock revolution they helped create has made a profound, and as yet not fully realized, change in the cultural and emotional attitudes of the generation that will come to power in the 1970s."

When contacted in 2004 to ask if he still stood by his 1978 rating of *Let It Bleed* as history's finest album, Greil Marcus replied, "Along with Bob Dylan's Highway 61 Revisited, I still think it's the greatest rock and roll album ever made, and 'Gimmie Shelter' [sic] is one of a few songs ('Like a Rolling Stone', 'One Fine Day', 'I Wonder Why', 'Johnny B. Goode', 'Complete Control', 'Whole Lotta Shakin' Goin' On', 'Lose Yourself') that while you're listening to it is the greatest single rock and roll recording imaginable." He also disagreed that the smutty lyrics have dated the album. "This was a platform of familiarity from which they could launch the assault contained in 'Gimme Shelter' and 'You Can't Always Get What You Want'. Hit the crowd in the face, then lull them into complacency, tell them everything's as it's always been, then hit them again."

Roy Carr, author of *The Rolling Stones: An Illustrated Record*, one of the best books on the band, disagrees, virtually dismissing it in his summary there. "Not so much another album as a collection of vignettes depicting the Stones faithfully playing out their accepted role as vandals, outlaws and satyrs."

Richie Unterberger, as ubiquitous a rock critic in his era as Marcus was in his, is about halfway between Marcus and Carr in his praise. *Writing in the All Music Guide To Rock,* he said, "this extends the rock & blues feel of *Beggars Banquet* into slightly harder-rocking, more demonically sexual territory. The Stones were never as consistent on album as their main rivals, the Beatles, and *Let It Bleed* suffers from some rather perfunctory tracks, like 'Monkey Man' and a countrified remake of the classic 'Honky Tonk Women' (here titled 'Country Honk'). Yet some of the songs are among their very best, especially 'Gimme Shelter,' with its shimmering guitar lines and apocalyptic lyrics; the harmonica-driven 'Midnight Rambler'; the druggy party ambience of the title track; and the stunning 'You Can't Always Get What You Want', which was the Stones' 'Hey Jude' of sorts, with its epic structure, horns, philosophical lyrics, and swelling choral vocals. 'You Got the Silver' (Keith Richards's first lead vocal) and Robert Johnson's 'Love in Vain', by contrast, were as close to the roots of acoustic down-home blues as the Stones ever got."

However, a consensus does seem to exist on "Gimme Shelter" constituting the band's magnum opus. Richards, interviewed for the issue of *Uncut* already mentioned in which it was voted by a panel of critics and musicians the greatest of all Stones tracks, said, "That being number one is very gratifying." Jagger, speaking in the same issue, nominated it as his all-time top Stones recording.

Whether or not it is their finest album, *Let It Bleed* was a fitting end to the era the Rolling Stones had helped shape, especially when set against *Abbey Road*, released just over two months earlier. The latter album was very, very pleasant and uncontroversial—just as The Beatles had mostly always been. *Let It Bleed* carried on the Stones' tradition of outrage and defiance. As The Beatles closed the decade in acrimony that would lead to their dissolution, the Stones were undergoing a renaissance, fired up by a new member and a comeback tour. How fitting then, that *Let It Bleed* should see them making a better album than The Beatles for the first time.

Keith Altham says, "I suppose you've got to say that Brian's departure and Mick Taylor's introduction did give them some sort of re-energizing. He played beautiful blues guitar. Brian's death, Mick's introduction, the fact that they had had a period in the doldrums meant that as far as Mick [Jagger] was concerned certainly they'd got something to prove and I suppose to that extent they were going to do it." He adds, "I also think that great albums are quite often produced in adversity and I think this was one of those situations where they'd gone through an awful lot. Out of that pain quite often great works are produced."

appendix 1
Vinyl Singles

(Listed by date or month of release)

Where only US or UK release
indicated in brackets.

7/6/63	Come On - I Want To Be Loved. [UK]	23/9/66	Have You Seen Your Mother, Baby, Standing In The Shadows - Who's Driving Your Plane?.
1/11/63	I Wanna Be Your Man - Stoned. [UK]		
21/2/64	Not Fade Away - Little By Little.	13/1/67	Let's Spend The Night Together - Ruby Tuesday.
26/6/64	It's All Over Now - Good Times Bad Times.	18/8/67	We Love You - Dandelion.
Aug 64	Tell Me - I Just Wanna Make Love To You. [US]	24/5/67	Jumping Jack Flash - Child Of The Moon.
Nov 64	Time Is On My Side - Congratulations. [US]	4/7/69	Honky Tonk Women - You Can't Always Get What You Want.
13/11/64	Little Red Rooster - Off The Hook. [UK]	16/4/71	Brown Sugar - Bitch - Let It Rock.
Jan 65	Heart Of Stone - What A Shame. [US]	14/4/72	Tumbling Dice - Sweet Black Angel.
26/2/65	The Last Time - Play With Fire.	20/8/73	Angie - Silver Train.
20/8/64	(I Can't Get No) Satisfaction - The Spider And The Fly.	July 74	It's Only Rock And Roll - Through The Lonely Nights.
22/10/65	Get Off Of My Cloud - The Singer Not The Song.	19/4/76	Fool To Cry - Crazy Mama.
Jan 66	As Tears Go By - Gotta Get Away. [US]	2/5/78	Miss You - Faraway Eyes.
4/2/66	19th Nervous Breakdown - As Tears Go By.	15/8/78	Beast Of Burden - When The Whip Comes Down. [US]
13/5/66	Paint It Black - Long Long While.	20/9/78	Respectable - When The Whip Comes Down.
		July 80	Emotional Rescue - Down In A Hole.

The twelve singles below were released in a boxed set Titled "Single Stones".

Sept 80	Come On - I Wanna Be Your Man.
Sept 80	It's All Over Now - I Want To Be Loved.
Sept 80	Satisfaction - Little By Little.
Sept 80	Not Fade Away - Little Red Rooster.
Sept 80	The Last Time - Paint It Black.
Sept 80	Get Off Of My Cloud - Play With Fire.
Sept 80	Jumping Jack Flash.
Sept 80	19th Nervous Breakdown - Have You Seen Your Mother, Baby, Standing In The Shadows.
Sept 80	Let's Spend The Night Together - You Can't Always Get What You Want.
Sept 80	Honky Tonk Women - Ruby Tuesday.
Sept 80	Street Fighting Man - Out Of Time.
26/9/80	She's So Cold - Send It To Me.
14/8/81	Start Me Up - No Use In Crying.
Dec 81	Waiting On A Friend - Little T&A.
Jun 82	Going To A Go-Go - Beast Of Burden.
Nov 83	Undercover Of The Night - All The Way Down.
Jan 84	She Was Hot - I Think I'm Going Mad.
Mar 86	Harlem Shuffle - Had It With You.
May 86	One Hit (To The Body) - Fight.
15/9/97	Anybody Seen My Baby.

appendix 2
CD Singles

(Listed by month of release)

Aug 89	Mixed Emotions - Fancyman Blues.
Nov 89	Rock And A Hard Place.
June 90	Almost Heard You Sigh - Wish I'd Never Met You.
July 90	Terrifying - Rock And A Hard Place.
Feb 91	Highwire - 2000 Light Years From Home.
June 91	Ruby Tuesday (Live).
July 94	Love Is Strong - The Storm.
Oct 94	Out Of Tears.
Oct 94	You Got Me Rocking - Jump On Top Of Me.

appendix 3
Vinyl Albums
(Listed by month of release)

Apr 64	The Rolling Stones.
Jan 65	The Rolling Stones No.2.
Sep 65	Out Of Our Heads.
Apr 66	Aftermath.
Nov 66	Big Hits - High Tide And Green Grass.
Jan 67	Between The Buttons.
Dec 67	Their Satanic Majesties Request.
Dec 68	Beggars Banquet.
Sep 69	Through The Past Darkly (Big Hits Volume 2).
Dec 69	Let It Bleed.
Sep 70	Get Yer Ya Ya's Out.
Apr 71	Stone Age.
Apr 71	Sticky Fingers.
May 72	Exile On Main St.
Aug 73	Goats Head Soup.
Oct 74	It's Only Rock 'N' Roll.
June 75	Made In The Shade.
Apr 76	Black And Blue.
Sep 77	Love You Live.
June 78	Some Girls.
June 80	Emotional Resue.
May 81	Sucking In The Seventies.
Sep 81	Tattoo You.
June 82	Still Life (American Concert 1981).
Apr 86	Dirty Work.

appendix 4
CD Albums

(Listed by month of release)

Jan 83	Beggars Banquet.	Nov 89	Still Life (American
Mar 85	Undercover.		Concert 1981).
Jul 84	The Rolling Stones.	Nov 89	Sucking In The Seventies.
Aoug 84	Out Of Our Heads.	Nov 89	Tattoo You.
Nov 84	12 * 5.	June 90	Hot Rocks 1964 - 1971.
May 85	Aftermath.	Oct 90	More Hot Rocks.
July 85	Between The Buttons.	Apr 91	Flashpoint.
Aug 85	Hot Rocks 1.	June 91	Big Hits (High Tide And
Aug 85	Hot Rocks 2.		Green Grass).
Feb 86	Their Satanic Majesties	June 91	Big Hits Volume 2.
	Request.	Nov 93	Jump Back.
Feb 86	Let It Bleed.	Aug 94	Voodoo Lounge.
May 86	Dirty Work.	Oct 95	Stripped
Aug 88	December's Children	Oct 96	Rock'n'Roll Circus
	(And Everybody's).	Oct 97	Bridges To Babylon
Aug 88	Flowers.	Nov 98	No Security
Aug 88	Get Yer Ya Ya's Out.	Oct 02	Forty Licks
Aug 88	Got Live If You Want It.	Nov 04	Live Licks
Aug 88	More Hot Rocks		
	Volume 1.		
Aug 88	The Rolling Stones, Now.		
Sep 89	Steel Wheels.		
Sep 89	Singles Collection - The		
	London Years.		
Nov 89	Black And Blue.		
Nov 89	Emotional Rescue.		
Nov 89	Exile On Main St.		
Nov 89	Goats Head Soup.		
Nov 89	It's Only Rock 'N' Roll.		
Nov 89	Love You Live.		
Nov 89	Made In The Shade.		
Nov 89	Rewind.		
Nov 89	Some Girls.		
Nov 89	Sticky Fingers.		

acknowledgments

My grateful thanks go to those who agreed to be interviewed for this book: Keith Altham, Bruce Botnick, Vic Coppersmith-Heaven, George Chkiantz, Dave Hassinger, Victor Kahn, Al Kooper, Greil Marcus, and Alan O'Duffy. I have also used quotes from a Bill Wyman interview I conducted in 2003.

I'd like to thank the following Stones experts for help with queries as well as providing clippings and recordings: Felix Aeppli, Christian Diemoz, Martin Elliott, Michael Lynch, Ian McPherson, and Chris Menicou.

Thanks also to Dawn Eden, Andrew Loog Oldham, and Richie Unterberger for help with queries.

The following websites were highly useful for discographical and/or sessionography information:

http://www.allmusic.com
http://www.frayed.org
http://mypage.bluewin.ch/aeppli/tug.htm#basic
http://www.nzentgraf.de
http://www.timeisonourside.com

The following books were all of use:

Appleford, Steve, *Rolling Stones: It's Only Rock 'N' Roll*, Schirmer Books, New York, 1998
Booth, Stanley, *True Adventures Of The Rolling Stones, A*

Cappella Publishing, Southwet Harbor, 2000

Carr, Roy, *The Rolling Stones: An Illustrated Record*, Random House, New York, 1977

Davis, Stephen, *Old Gods Almost Dead: the 40-year Odyssey of the Rolling Stones*, Aurum Press, London, 2002,

Elliott, Martin, *The Rolling Stones Complete Recording Sessions 1962-2002*, Cherry Red Books, London, 2002

Faithfull, Marianne & Dalton, David, *Faithfull*, Penguin Books, London, 1995

Gambaccini, Paul, *Critics Choice Top 200 Albums*, Omnibus Press, London, 1978

Hector, James, *The Complete Guide To The Music Of The Rolling Stones*, Omnibus Press, London, 1995

Jagger, Mick, Richards, Keith, Watts, Charlie, & Wood, Ronnie, *According To The Rolling Stones*, Weidenfeld & Nicolson, London, 2003

Norman, Philip, *The Stones*, Sidgwick & Jackson, London, 2001

Salewicz, Chris, *Mick and Keith: Parallel Lines*, Orion, London, 2002

Sanchez, Tony & Blake, John, *Up And Down With The Rolling Stones*, Blake Publishing, London 1991

Wyman, Bill, *Rolling With The Stones*, Dorling Kindersley, London, 2002

Wyman Bill & Coleman, Ray, *Stone Alone: The Story of a Rock Band*, Penguin Books, London, 2002

index